PENGUIN  CLASSICS

PROMETHEUS BOUND
AND OTHER PLAYS

ADVISORY EDITOR: BETTY RADICE

AESCHYLUS was born of a noble family at Eleusis near Athens in 525 B.C. He took part in the Persian Wars and his epitaph, said to have been written by himself, represents him as fighting at Marathon. At some time in his life he appears to have been prosecuted for divulging the Eleusinian mysteries, but he apparently proved himself innocent. Aeschylus wrote more than seventy plays, of which seven have survived: *The Suppliants*, *The Persians*, *Seven Against Thebes*, *Prometheus Bound*, *Agamemnon*, *The Choephori* and *The Eumenides*. (All translated by Philip Vellacott for the Penguin Classics.) He visited Syracuse more than once at the invitation of Hieron I and he died at Gela in Sicily in 456 B.C. Aeschylus was recognized as a classic writer soon after his death, and special privileges were decreed for his plays.

PHILIP VELLACOTT is the translator of several volumes for the Penguin Classics; these are works by Aeschylus, Euripides, Menander and Theophrastus. He was educated at St Paul's School and Magdalene College, Cambridge, and for twenty-five years he taught classics (and drama for twelve years) at Dulwich College. He has lectured on Greek drama on four tours in the U.S.A. and from 1967 to 1968 he was Visiting Lecturer at the University of California at Santa Cruz. Philip Vellacott, who is married, is also the author of several plays, mostly on Greek subjects, *Sophocles and Oedipus* (1971), and *Ironic Drama: A Study of Euripides' Method and Meaning* (1975).

D0059355

AESCHYLUS

PROMETHEUS BOUND
THE SUPPLIANTS
SEVEN AGAINST THEBES
THE PERSIANS

TRANSLATED WITH AN INTRODUCTION BY
PHILIP VELLACOTT

PENGUIN BOOKS

Penguin Books Ltd, Harmondsworth, Middlesex, England
Viking Penguin Inc., 40 West 23rd Street, New York, New York 10010, U.S.A.
Penguin Books Australia Ltd, Ringwood, Victoria, Australia
Penguin Books Canada Limited, 2801 John Street, Markham, Ontario, Canada L3R 1B4
Penguin Books (N.Z.) Ltd, 182–190 Wairau Road, Auckland 10, New Zealand

—

This translation first published 1961
Reprinted 1964, 1968, 1970, 1971, 1973, 1975, 1976, 1978,
1979, 1980, 1981, 1982, 1983, 1984, 1986, 1987

—

—

Made and printed in Great Britain by
Hazell Watson & Viney Limited,
Member of the BPCC Group,
Aylesbury, Bucks
Set in Monotype Perpetua

CONTENTS

INTRODUCTION

AESCHYLUS wrote altogether over seventy plays, of which seven have survived; and of these the Oresteian Trilogy probably came last, being produced within two years of the poet's death. This volume contains the other four; and the order in which they are given is probably the reverse of their chronological order. *Prometheus* is put first because it is the best known to English readers. Though its date is uncertain, the style suggests that it belongs to the mature period. *The Suppliants* follows because its story is foretold in *Prometheus*. It was until fairly recently regarded as the earliest of all; but opinion has changed and now places it among the later works, about 463 B.C. Both these plays belong to trilogies which, like the Oresteia, present a struggle between opposing rights or principles, and trace its course through successive crises to its solution in a rational compromise. *Seven Against Thebes* (467 B.C.) illustrates an earlier stage. The Oedipus Trilogy of which it is the last act shows the working-out of a family curse like that of the House of Atreus, but ends simply with the annihilation of the family; there is no reconciliation, no solution. *The Persians* is the earliest (472 B.C.) and was produced only eight years after the historical event which it records, the Battle of Salamis; and its subject-matter puts it in a class by itself.

PROMETHEUS BOUND AND THE SUPPLIANTS

'The kindness of the enthroned gods contains an element of force.' This phrase, the more striking because of its echo in the New Testament, occurs in the first great choral ode of *Agamemnon*, at the close of a passage which states in a few memorable lines the essence of Aeschylus' belief about 'the ways of God to man'. God, the playwright says, is concerned that man should learn wisdom, and has marked out the path; and it is a path of suffering. Men are in one sense free to learn or not to learn; but the painful condition of learning is inexorable. The nature of God, in other words, comprises two elements or principles, one harsh, the other gentle. The third play of the Oresteian Trilogy, *The Eumenides*, has for its theme the reconciliation of these two principles, of revenge with justice, of force with persuasion.

Prometheus and *The Suppliants* both open, broadly speaking, the same theme. Each is the first play of a trilogy; and each presents the operation of violence. The second and third plays of both trilogies are lost; but the evidence available for guessing their contents suggests (at least in the case of *The Suppliants*) more or less what the analogy of the Oresteia would lead us to expect: that the second play showed the result of violence in breeding further violence, while the third brought two opposed sides together in a reasoned reconciliation. The second and third plays of the Promethean Trilogy were *Prometheus Unbound* and *Prometheus the Fire-Bringer*. Unfortunately the few remains of these plays are too fragmentary to give any clue to details of the way in which Aeschylus unfolded his theme. The two sequels to *The Suppliants* were *The Egyptians* and *The Danaids*; and the trilogy is usually referred to as the Danaid Trilogy. Here the probabilities are somewhat clearer, as will be seen presently.

The Eumenides presented the struggle between Violence and Reason as embodied in the heroes and gods of the Homeric age, though closely linked to living issues of the fifth century B.C. In *Prometheus* we are taken still further back, to the first phase of the same struggle, to a period which, historically, is that of the first appearance in Greece of the 'Olympian' gods, but which Greeks thought of as belonging to the most primitive stage of the history of man.

The transition from the primitive to the civilized world, from the life of nomadic tribes and village settlements to that of walled cities and organized states, was doubtless a gradual and barely perceptible process spread confusedly over several centuries and large expanses of land. Individuals who noted such change, however, must generally have associated it with some sudden or memorable event – an invasion, a siege, a massacre, a migration. So this stage in the development of Greek social order had its mythical counterpart in the story of a violent dynastic change among the gods.

In the primitive era Cronos was lord of all gods. During his time the human race was created, but was early recognized as a regrettable failure, and kept in a state of wretchedness and total subservience. Force ruled everything; reason and right were unknown. The Titans, sons of Earth begotten by gods, were a race of gigantic size and strength, and no intelligence; until in one of them, Prometheus, emerged rational and moral qualities, ranging from cunning and ingenuity to a love of freedom and justice. The knowledge that the future lay with such intangible principles rather than with brute strength, was a secret possessed by Earth, who imparted it to her son Prometheus. (The earth was in all centuries thought of by the Greeks as the prime source of foreknowledge and prophecy.) This certainty set Prometheus at the side of Zeus, son of Cronos, in rebellion against his father and the older dynasty; and by Prometheus' help Zeus and the other 'Olympian' gods won the day and thenceforward ruled the universe.

But Prometheus was not only an immortal; he was also a son of Earth, and felt a natural sympathy with the earth's mortal inhabitants. The race which Zeus despised and planned to destroy, Prometheus saw as capable of infinite development. He stole fire from heaven and gave it to them; and he taught them the basic mental and manual skills. In so doing he frustrated Zeus's plan to create a more perfect race. So when Aeschylus shows him punished for this presumption, the reader or spectator, judging between the antagonists, finds the scales nicely balanced. What wins our favour for Prometheus is largely the fact that he believed in, and wanted to help, the human race as it is, full of both noble achievement and pitiable squalor, honouring both goodness and wickedness; a race where virtue, if rare, is at least costly. But though in this play the balance of feeling is in favour of Prometheus, even the sympathetic Chorus rebuke him for pride: and it is clear that Zeus's case has still to be presented.

This must have been done in *Prometheus Unbound*. (Indeed it is hard to see what material was left for the third play.) There can be little doubt that by the end of the trilogy Zeus himself abandoned the use of force and opened negotiations with Prometheus, who then told him of the prophecy concerning the sea-nymph Thetis; that Heracles, with the permission of Zeus, set Prometheus free, perhaps first shooting the eagle with his bow; that the Centaur Chiron, longing for death in the agonies of the wound Heracles had inflicted, was allowed to lose his immortality and descend to Hades, thus 'taking on himself the pains of Prometheus' in fulfilment of prophecy (see page 51, and note, page 154); and that the final settlement recognized the supremacy of Zeus, the right of the human race to exist and develop, and the superiority of reason to violence.

The longest scene in the play is that in which Io, the virgin daughter of Inachus king of Argos, visits Prometheus and gains his sympathy as a fellow-victim of the tyranny of Zeus. This scene occupies more than 300 lines in the middle of the action. A large part of it is taken up with descriptions of the hazardous journeys which Io is fated to undertake before she finally becomes the bride of Zeus. Aeschylus lived in an age of travel and exploration, and it is natural that his writing, like Shakespeare's, should reflect his countrymen's intense interest in tales of distant regions and strange tribes. But the story of Io is used also to hint, even at this early stage in the drama, that there is another side to the character of Zeus, which time will reveal. Once Io reaches Egypt, Prometheus says,

> Here at last Zeus shall restore your mind, and come
> Upon you, not with terror, with a gentle touch.

Whether the end of Io's sufferings had any part in the two other plays can only be guessed; there is no evidence of it. But it is clear that *Prometheus Unbound* had for its leading character Heracles, the descendant of Io, whose fame as a benefactor of mankind rivalled that of Prometheus.

As the story of Io constitutes the background for the whole action of *The Suppliants*, it should now be told in full. As daughter of the king of Argos she was priestess in the temple of Hera, the patron goddess of that city. Zeus saw and desired her; and Hera, in this instance becoming aware of the attachment before a union had been achieved, used more than usual thoroughness in the steps she took to prevent it. She transformed Io into a cow; and provided an immortal herdsman, a giant named Argus (which means 'sharp-eyed'), to watch her day and night. Zeus commanded Hermes to kill Argus; whereupon Hera sent a gadfly to madden Io with its sting and drive her in torment from country to country. The prolonged and innocent sufferings of Io give her, in spite of the grotesque form they assumed, a special pathos, and a place of special interest among the many mothers of Zeus's children. At last, by way of Thrace, the Bosphorus, Asia Minor, and Phoenicia, Io reached Egypt. There Hera's cruelty ceased to pursue her; the madness induced by the gadfly left her; her human form was fully or partly restored – though versions of the legend vary. There too Zeus, whose love for her had been decreed by Fate for fulfilment, visited her, and made her pregnant by the breath of his nostrils and the touch of his hand. Again, it is not clear whether this unusual consummation is to be connected with Io's metamorphosis or regarded as a sensitive expression of tenderness towards an afflicted woman. Io bore Zeus a son, Epaphos, whose name means 'a touch'.

It is evident that this story is of great anthropological interest, and has connexions with early Egyptian religious ideas; but here we are concerned with its subsequent episodes, which provide the plot of the Danaid Trilogy. Epaphos and his descendants lived by the River Nile, where, three generations later, the family was represented by two brothers, Aegyptus and Danaus. Aegyptus had fifty sons, Danaus fifty daughters. The youths determined to marry their cousins; whereupon the daughters of Danaus (that is, the Danaides or Danaids) fled, under the guidance of their father, to Argos, the original home of their ancestress Io. The sons of Aegyptus pursued them; but the king and people of Argos gave them sanctuary and defied the Egyptians. At this point *The Suppliants* ends.

The outline of subsequent events as given by the legend says that Danaus finally persuaded his daughters to agree to the marriage – but there was treachery in the agreement, planned and directed by Danaus. He made all his daughters swear an oath together to murder their bridegrooms on the wedding night. All performed their oaths, except one: Hypermestra found the claims of love stronger than those of loyalty to the pact made with her sisters, and spared her husband Lynceus. To us, this is the point where the story becomes most interesting; but early tradition says as little about the further adventures of Hypermestra as it does about Orestes. This was fortunate for Aeschylus, as it gave him freedom in the construction of his trilogy; but how he used this freedom we can only conjecture. One considerable fragment survives from the third play, *The Danaids*. It is part of a speech by Aphrodite, and runs as follows:

> The holy heaven is full of desire to mate with the earth, and desire seizes the earth to find a mate; rain falls from the amorous heaven and impregnates the earth; and the earth brings forth for men the fodder of flocks and herds and the gifts of Demeter; and from the same moistening marriage-rite the fruit of trees is ripened. Of these things I am the cause.

This speech, which clearly extols love as the essential principle of life in the universe, may be taken to show that Aphrodite defended Hyper-mestra's action in sparing Lynceus, and persuaded the forty-nine sisters to be reconciled to the prospect of marriage. Later writers, as might be expected, said that the Danaids eventually found husbands, whose natural apprehensions proved groundless; while Hypermestra and Lynceus became ancestors of the kings of Argos.

How does Aeschylus treat this exciting but intractable material?* To begin with, he gives a clearly marked character to his collective heroine, the Chorus of Danaids. Whereas the sons of Aegyptus, by disposition and instinct, are more allied to their barbarian than to their Greek ancestry, being lustful, violent, and aggressive, the Danaids by contrast are civilized in their aspirations; though under stress of an emergency their thoughts are ready to embrace violence in a reckless and even impious form. Next, the character of Danaus, crafty and de-termined, is carefully prepared in the first play for the bloodthirsty and unscrupulous role assigned to him in the second; perhaps also for the fate he is to meet in the third, where he may well have suffered death for his conspiracy to murder. But, most important, Aeschylus gives a clearer and more relevant presentation of the central moral issue than that provided by the legend. The legend said that the Danaids regarded the proposed union as incestuous. Aeschylus mentions this view in the course of the play; but, since Athenians of his day felt no objection to marriage between cousins, he does not emphasize it, but transfers interest to another aspect of the matter, namely the aggressive be-haviour of the sons of Aegyptus, who were proposing to take their cousins by force. Here, as in *The Eumenides*, reason and persuasion are put forward as the proper principles of civilized life. But they are principles which always find it difficult to defend themselves against the onslaught of violence. At the end of *The Suppliants* the Herald of the Egyptians declares war against Argos; and the Egyptian army has already landed.

A study of the text of *The Suppliants*, together with the fragment of Aphrodite's speech just mentioned, makes it possible to guess roughly what happened in the other two plays. It is probable that *The Egyptians* began with the defeat of the Argive army, perhaps the seige of the city.

* For ideas contained in these three paragraphs I am largely indebted to an article entitled 'The Danaid Trilogy', by Professor R. P. Winnington-Ingram, *Journal of Hellenic Studies*, vol. LXXXI, 1961.

It must have included the negotiations for the marriage, and had for its climax the plot to murder the fifty bridegrooms. The exodus at the end of the play may well have been a bridal march to the fatal marriage-chambers. The violence used by the Egyptians in the first play breeds the violence of their victims in the second. The outrage against Zeus God of Suppliants (*Zeus Hikesios*) is followed by the outrage against Zeus God of Hospitality (*Zeus Xenios*).

The third play must have opened with the discovery of the forty-nine murders, and the declaration of Hypermestra that she had spared her husband for love. This is a situation with which the State of Argos must deal; for the murder of the city's guests has brought pollution and will invite revenge. But Danaus and forty-nine of his daughters will certainly regard Hypermestra as the criminal and traitress, and Lynceus as the enemy. Decision must lie with the Argive Assembly, who in *The Suppliants* condemned the defiance of Zeus Hikesios, and will now surely condemn the defiance of Zeus Xenios. But if the Danaids are condemned for their crime, what of the pity which we felt for them in the first play, when they were helpless victims? What is to happen to them? It is this dilemma which requires divine intervention in the person of Aphrodite. How she solved it we do not know; but the solution most likely included both their reconciliation to marriage and their purification from blood-guilt; and illustrated again the belief that Zeus combines force with benevolence in teaching human beings the right path of life.

Before we leave *The Suppliants* a few minor points should be mentioned. First, the number of the Chorus. The legend said there were fifty Danaids. If there were fifty in this Chorus, there must have been fifty maids attending them; and the number of soldiers who came with the Egyptian Herald can hardly, in that case, have been less than twenty. That means that King Pelasgus must have arrived with a guard of at least thirty, if he was to appear easily able to overpower the Egyptians. Then Danaus' bodyguard must have been large enough not to look small beside that of the king. It is quite possible that a large crowd like this was the poet's intention; though it would seem more suitable at the end of a trilogy (as in *The Eumenides*) than at the beginning. Certainly when Tragedy first began the Chorus numbered fifty; and at an unknown date this number was reduced to twelve, as in *Agamemnon*. It was partly because of this that *The Suppliants* used to be thought a very early work; if, however, the true date is 463 or thereabouts, it seems unwise to be dogmatic about the number of the Chorus.

Whatever their number, when the Chorus-Leader is speaking of herself and her fellows, she follows the convention of Tragedy in using nearly always the first person singular. In the translation the first person plural has generally been used, except where the singular seemed suitable in the context.

The name Aegyptus needs a brief comment. Plainly he is an 'eponymous hero' invented as a father to the race of Egyptians. I have used the Latin spelling for his name, and the English spelling for the land of Egypt.

SEVEN AGAINST THEBES

The story of Oedipus and his family, which is best known from the Theban plays of Sophocles, belongs to the generation which preceded that of the siege of Troy. Like the story of Agamemnon, it traces the working-out of a curse which fell upon a family, and which renewed itself by the rashness and impiety of successive generations. Unlike the Oresteia, however, it bears no hopeful message of 'redemption from within'; the curse exhausts itself only with the extinction of the family.

When the play opens Oedipus is already dead. His two sons, Eteocles and Polyneices, have quarrelled. We gather that there had been an agreement between them to share equally the kingly power inherited from their father; but Eteocles had contrived to seize sole power for himself, whereupon Polyneices had sought help from Adrastus king of Argos and six other kings, and had brought a large and mixed force to attack his native city.

But the brothers had quarrelled also with Oedipus before he died. The ground of this quarrel is not clear; but it had something to do with the way in which they looked after their father and maintained him from the day when the truth about his incestuous marriage was disclosed, and he blinded himself. Enraged at their attitude to him, Oedipus had cursed them; and included in his curse was the prediction that 'a stranger coming from the sea, born of fire, should prove a harsh divider of inheritance for them'. In the course of the play this riddle is expounded. The 'stranger' is iron, a metal newly imported from Pontus (*pontus* is a Greek word for 'sea'); and with iron, hardened in the fire and sharpened, Eteocles and Polyneices divide their inheritance.

The curse goes back still further. It was first incurred by Laius, Oedipus' father. He had been warned by Apollo that a son of his would kill him, and commanded to live and die childless. His disobedience earned the enmity of Apollo. He tried to remedy his fault by getting rid of his infant child; with what result is well known, the story being immortalized in Sophocles' *King Oedipus*. In *Seven Against Thebes* Eteocles is deeply aware of the curse on his family, and in particular of the curse of Oedipus, which haunts him in dreams. In the activity and excitement of preparing for battle he forgets gloomy forebodings, and shows in his attitude to the enemy's threats a proper modesty and recognition of the gods. One by one he dispatches his six most notable warriors to meet the attack of the kings at six of the seven gates of Thebes.

When only he himself is left, the Messenger tells him that at the seventh gate the attack is led by his brother Polyneices. Both Messenger and Chorus appear to assume that Eteocles, to avoid shedding kindred blood, will send for another champion, or alter the disposition already made. His refusal to do so is not due merely to his fear of seeming afraid to fight his brother, nor to the loss of face entailed in counter-manding his dispositions. It is due to his Greek sense of tragedy, to his conviction that destiny cannot be avoided. When he hears that his brother is at the seventh gate he feels that the curse has caught up with him. He tells himself that by a shuffle on this occasion he may avoid it; but it will find him again, perhaps in a still more terrifying manifesta-tion. There is, there can be, no escape.

That is how Eteocles sees the situation. The Chorus see another side to it. If Eteocles will only exercise the modesty and piety he has hitherto shown, and change gates with one of the six champions, all may yet be well. The anger of the gods which now rages hotly may pass in time; to commit kindred murder now is to despair of any end to the curse, and to justify any doom which Heaven may bring upon the city. In other words, the Chorus feel that, though the curse is a reality, the fate of the house of Oedipus lies at this moment in the choice of Eteocles. He, being the man he is, and the son of Oedipus, will act impulsively and make the wrong choice; but the possibility of right choice exists, and justifies the gods. Aeschylus does not specifically pose this issue of free will, but it is surely there in the text, just as it is in *Agamemnon*.

There is very little action in the play. About one-third of its length is occupied by the scene in which the Messenger describes each champion of the invading army, his weapons, and his character. The first five are inordinately arrogant, and this gives Eteocles confidence that the gods cannot be on their side. The sixth, Amphiaraus, is modest, reluctant to take part in the war, and pious. This gives more cause for concern; but Eteocles appoints Lasthenes to meet him, and commits the issue to the gods. After this comes the climax, the revelation that Polyneices is at the seventh gate. That is as much as can be found of dramatic pattern in this long and static scene. However, not only is there much vivid imagery and moving speech in every episode, and in the choral songs, but in the play as a whole an added interest appears when it is realized that a current issue of Athenian policy is clearly and strongly dealt with. This is above all a play, as Aristophanes says in *The Frogs*, full of martial spirit, a play about the successful defence of a strongly walled city. It was produced in 467 B.C. only twelve years after the Persians had left Athens a desolate ruin. Far-sighted Athenian leaders had repeatedly urged their fellow-citizens at whatever cost to surround Athens with impregnable walls; for her rising power was already making enemies in Greece itself. There is little doubt that many phrases in the play would convey to the audience the poet's urgent warning to be wise in time. Within a year or two after its production the fortification of the Acropolis was begun in earnest.

Seven Against Thebes is the third play of a trilogy, of which the first was *Laius*, the second *Oedipus*. The brilliance and popularity of Sophocles' *King Oedipus* must account for the disappearance of Aeschylus' play on the same subject; but it is clear from references in this play that Aeschylus followed in general the outline of the story as we know it. Unfortunately the text of the play is not as Aeschylus left it. Fifty years or more after his death, when Sophocles' *Antigone* was among the most notable pieces in the Athenian repertory, a new ending was written for Aeschylus' play, introducing Antigone and Ismene, the proclamation forbidding burial to Polyneices, and Antigone's defiance. This spurious ending is well written, and an English audience might feel that it saved a dull play at the last moment. But the poet's intention was undoubtedly to end the play with the mourning over the two brothers. With their deaths the family is extinct and the curse fulfilled; and the sisters are irrelevant. Their scene, which introduces a new chapter in the story, can have no place in the third play of a trilogy.

Since, however, the original ending – perhaps some twenty or fifty lines – is lost, there is nothing for it but to translate the play as it stands in the manuscripts.

THE PERSIANS

This is the only Greek play besides the comedies whose subject-matter was taken not from legend but from recent history. It was produced in 472 B.C., eight years after the Battle of Salamis. The scene is the court of the king of Persia, and the action is simply the arrival of a messenger with news of the Persian defeat, and the subsequent arrival of King Xerxes, broken-spirited and disgraced. The purpose of the play was the gratification of the natural pride of the Athenians in their achievement, and the presentation of the victory of Salamis as the focal moment in the defeat of Persia and the establishment of Greek liberty. That victory was undoubtedly of first importance and made everything else possible; and it was due almost entirely to the united courage and resolution of the Athenian people. The repulse of the Persians was completed the following year at the Battle of Plataea. This victory was the achievement of Sparta, and the Athenian force seems to have played a feeble part in it, quite possibly through jealousy. Thus it would have been at least irrelevant to mention Plataea in the Messenger's scene. It is given a fair, though brief, prophetic mention by the Ghost of Darius as the *coup de grâce* to the Persian expedition, and is duly credited to the Dorians, which means the Spartans. It is unfair to Aeschylus to say that he belittles the importance of Plataea. His theme is the victory of Athens; his audience were his fellow-citizens. He was writing his play inside Athens, himself deeply involved in the creative fever of ambition which was driving the Athenians forward to liberty, expansion and supremacy; and the occasion of its performance was religious, a national thanksgiving by Athenians for Athens.

The Messenger's speech (page 13ff.) is in fact the earliest account we have of the Battle of Salamis; and as it is almost certain that Aeschylus himself either watched or took part in the battle, his account must be treated seriously as a historical document. It does, however, show considerable discrepancies with the other fifth-century account, in the eighth book of Herodotus. In comparing the two and assessing the probable reliability of each, most readers would conclude that the points are about even. Aeschylus certainly knew the facts, and presented his play before thousands who could refute him if he was wrong. On the other hand, his and his audience's concern was with poetry, ritual, and celebration rather than with history. Herodotus was interested in the idea of history and in telling a good story; he too had strong ties with Athens, and his account of the Battle of Plataea shows him to be far from impartial. In any case he had to rely on casual records and fading or inventive memories.

Aeschylus was known for his love of spectacle; and it is reasonable to suppose that the effect of this play was enhanced by a lavish variety of Oriental costume and by an attempt to represent the manners, and perhaps the speech, of the defeated enemy – an entertainment for victors such as Shakespeare provided in *King Henry V*. There are evidences of this in the text: the long lists of magnificently outlandish names, half a dozen Persian words, and some Chorus-rhythms associated with Eastern music. (The raising of the ghost of Darius can perhaps not be regarded merely as an oriental extravagance, since the ghost of Clytemnestra appears in *The Eumenides*; though necromancy was in fact not included in the usual Greek methods of divination.) But there is no real plot. Apart from the pageantry and the poetry the chief interest must have lain in the splendid vividness of the Messenger's narrative.

*

For *The Suppliants*, *Seven Against Thebes*, and *The Persians* I have used mainly the editions of T. G. Tucker; for *Prometheus* that of Sikes and Willson. The line-numbering used is that of the Oxford Classical Text.

PROMETHEUS BOUND

PROMETHEUS BOUND

*

CHARACTERS:

STRENGTH

VIOLENCE

HEPHAESTUS, *the God of Fire*

PROMETHEUS

CHORUS *of the Daughters of Oceanus*

OCEANUS, *the God of the Sea*

IO, *a Priestess of Argos*

HERMES, *Messenger of Zeus*

*

A rocky mountain-top, within sight of the sea.
Enter STRENGTH *and* VIOLENCE, *dragging in* PROMETHEUS.*
  HEPHAESTUS *follows.*

STRENGTH: Here we have reached the remotest region of the
    earth,
  The haunt of Scythians, a wilderness without a footprint.
  Hephaestus, do your duty. Remember what command
  The Father laid on you. Here is Prometheus, the rebel:
  Nail him to the rock; secure him on this towering summit
  Fast in the unyielding grip of adamantine chains.
  It was your treasure that he stole, the flowery splendour
  Of all-fashioning fire, and gave to men – an offence
  Intolerable to the gods, for which he now must suffer,
  Till he be taught to accept the sovereignty of Zeus
  And cease acting as champion of the human race.
HEPHAESTUS: For you two, Strength and Violence, the com-
    mand of Zeus
  Is now performed. You are released. But how can I

  * An asterisk indicates a Note at the end of the book, p. 153 ff.

20

Find heart to lay hands on a god of my own race,
And cruelly clamp him to this bitter, bleak ravine?
And yet I must; heart or no heart, this I must do.
To slight what Zeus has spoken is a fearful thing.
[*to* PROMETHEUS] Son of sagacious Themis, god of moun-
  tainous thoughts,
With heart as sore as yours I now shall fasten you
In bands of bronze immovable to this desolate peak,
Where you will hear no voice, nor see a human form;
But scorched with the sun's flaming rays your skin will lose
Its bloom of freshness. Glad you will be to see the night
Cloaking the day with her dark spangled robe; and glad
Again when the sun's warmth scatters the frost at dawn.
Each changing hour will bring successive pain to rack
Your body; and no man yet born shall set you free.
Your kindness to the human race has earned you this.
A god who would not bow to the gods' anger – you,
Transgressing right, gave privileges to mortal men.
For that you shall keep watch upon this bitter rock,
Standing upright, unsleeping, never bowed in rest.
And many groans and cries of pain shall come from you,
All useless; for the heart of Zeus is hard to appease.
Power newly won is always harsh.

STRENGTH: What is the use
  Of wasting time in pity? Why do you not hate
  A god who is an enemy to all the gods,
  Who gave away to humankind your privilege?

HEPHAESTUS: The ties of birth and comradeship are strangely
  strong.

STRENGTH: True, yet how is it possible to disobey
  The Father's word? Is not that something you dread more?

HEPHAESTUS: You have been always cruel, full of aggressive-
  ness.

STRENGTH: It does no good to break your heart for him. Come
  now,

You cannot help him: waste no time in worrying.

HEPHAESTUS: I hate my craft, I hate the skill of my own hands.

STRENGTH: Why do you hate it? Take the simple view: your craft

Is not to blame for what must be inflicted now.

HEPHAESTUS: True – yet I wish some other had been given my skill.

STRENGTH: All tasks are burdensome – except to rule the gods.

No one is free but Zeus.

HEPHAESTUS: I know. All this [indicating PRO-METHEUS] is proof

Beyond dispute.

STRENGTH: Be quick, then; put the fetters on him

Before the Father sees you idling.

HEPHAESTUS: Here, then, look!

The iron wrist-bands are ready. [he begins to fix them]

STRENGTH: Take them; manacle him;

Hammer with all your force, rivet him to the rock.

HEPHAESTUS: All right, I'm doing it! There, that iron will not come loose.

STRENGTH: Drive it in further; clamp him fast, leave nothing slack.

HEPHAESTUS: This arm is firm; at least he'll find no way out there.

STRENGTH: Now nail his other arm securely. Let him learn

That all his wisdom is but folly before Zeus.

HEPHAESTUS: There! None – but he – could fairly find fault with my work.

STRENGTH: Now drive straight through his chest with all the force you have

The unrelenting fang of the adamantine wedge.

HEPHAESTUS: Alas! I weep, Prometheus, for your sufferings.

STRENGTH: Still shrinking? Weeping for the enemy of Zeus?

Take care; or you may need your pity for yourself.

HEPHAESTUS *drives in the wedge.*

HEPHAESTUS: There! Now you see a sight to pain your eyes.

STRENGTH: I see
   Prometheus getting his deserts. Come, fix these girths
   Around his ribs.

HEPHAESTUS: I must. Don't drive me with commands.

STRENGTH: I swear I *will* command you – yes, and hound you
      on.
   Come lower down now; force his legs into this ring.

HEPHAESTUS: That's quickly done.

STRENGTH: Now nail those shackles
      fast. Hit hard!
   Our work has a stern judge.

HEPHAESTUS: Your speech matches your looks.

STRENGTH [*jeering*]: Be soft, then. But if I am hard and pitiless,
   Don't cast it at me.

HEPHAESTUS: Come, his legs are safe; let's go.
                    Exit HEPHAESTUS.

STRENGTH [*to* PROMETHEUS]: Stay there, and swell with
      upstart arrogance; and steal
   The privileges of gods to give to mortal men.
   How are your mortals going to cut *this* knot for you?
   You're wrongly named, Prometheus, Wise-before-the-event!
   Wisdom is just the thing you want, if you've a mind
   To squirm your way out of this blacksmith's masterpiece!
                 Exeunt STRENGTH *and* VIOLENCE.

PROMETHEUS: O divinity of sky, and swift-winged winds, and
      leaping streams,
   O countless laughter of the sea's waves,
   O Earth, mother of all life!
   On you, and on the all-seeing circle of the sun, I call:
   See what is done by gods to me, a god!

   See with what outrage
   Racked and tortured
   I am to agonize

For a thousand years!
See this shameful prison
Invented for me
By the new master of the gods!
I groan in anguish
For pain present and pain to come:
Where shall I see rise
The star of my deliverance?

What am I saying? I know exactly every thing
That is to be; no torment will come unforeseen.
My appointed fate I must endure as best I can,
Knowing the power of Necessity is irresistible.
Under such suffering, speech and silence are alike
Beyond me. For bestowing gifts upon mankind
I am harnessed in this torturing clamp. For I am he
Who hunted out the source of fire, and stole it, packed
In pith of a dry fennel-stalk. And fire has proved
For men a teacher in every art, their grand resource.
That was the sin for which I now pay the full price,
Bared to the winds of heaven, bound and crucified.

Ah! Who is there?
What sound, what fragrant air
Floats by me – whence, I cannot see?
From god, or man, or demigod?
Have you come to this peak at the world's end
To gaze at my torment? Or for what?
See me, a miserable prisoner,
A god, the enemy of Zeus,
Who have earned the enmity of all gods
That frequent the court of Zeus
Because I was too good a friend to men.

Ah, ah! I hear it again, close to me!
A rustling – is it of birds?
And the air whispering with the light beat of wings!

24

Whatever comes, brings fear.

Enter the CHORUS *in a winged ship or carriage.*

CHORUS: Fear nothing. We are all your friends.
We have flown to this mountain on racing wings,
Winning reluctant leave from our father;
And the winds carried us swiftly along.
For the echo of ringing steel
Shivered through the depths of our cave,
Shaking quiet bashfulness out of our thoughts;
And barefoot as we were
We came at once in our winged carriage.

PROMETHEUS: Alas, alas! Children of fertile Tethys,
Daughters of Oceanus, whose unsleeping tide
Encircles the whole earth, look at me.
See in how cruel a grip,
Pinned on the craggy peak of this ravine,
I must endure my fearful watch.

CHORUS: I look, Prometheus; and sudden fear fills my eyes
To see your body withering on this rock,
Outraged with fetters of adamant.
A new master holds the helm of Olympus;
These are new laws indeed
By which Zeus tyrannically rules;
And the great powers of the past he now destroys.

PROMETHEUS: Would that Zeus had sunk me under the earth,
Down below Hades, haven of the dead,
Into the immensity of Tartarus,
Fastening me in cruel fetters inextricably,
That no god or any other creature
Might feel glad to see me suffer.
Instead I am the miserable sport of every wind,
And my torments bring joy to my enemies.

CHORUS: What god is cruel-hearted enough
To find joy in such a sight?
Who does not suffer with you in your pain –

25

Save Zeus? He, firm in inflexible anger,
Treads down the race of Ouranos, and will not relent
Till his passion is sated, or till some cunning plot
Wrests from his hand his impregnable empire.

PROMETHEUS: I swear to you that I, humiliated as I am,
Bound hand and foot in these strong straps,
Shall yet be needed by the lord of immortals
To disclose the new design, tell him who it is
Shall rob him of his power and his glory.
The honied spells of his persuasive tongue shall not enchant me,
Nor shall I cower under his fierce threats, or tell this secret,
Until he free me from these brutal bonds
And consent to compensate me for his outrage.

CHORUS: You are defiant, Prometheus, and your spirit,
In spite of all your pain, yields not an inch.
But there is too much freedom in your words.
My heart is shaken with a piercing terror;
I tremble at your fate: how are you to reach
The end of these troubles and rest in a safe port?
For the son of Cronos is unapproachable in temper,
And no words can soften his heart.

PROMETHEUS: Zeus, I know, is ruthless,
And keeps law within his own will.
Nevertheless his temper shall in time turn mild,
When my words come true and he is broken.
Then at last he will calm his merciless anger,
And ask for a pact of friendship with me;
And I shall welcome him.

CHORUS: Now disclose everything and explain to us
Upon what charge Zeus had you seized
And treated with such ignominy and brutality.
Tell us, if telling involves no harm for you.

PROMETHEUS: To speak of this is painful for me; to keep
    silence
Is no less pain. On every side is suffering.

When first among the immortal gods anger broke out
Dividing them into two factions, of which one
Resolved to unseat the power of Cronos, and make Zeus
Absolute king – mark that! – while the opposing side
Resolved no less that Zeus should never rule the gods –
At that time I, offering the best of all advice,
Tried to convince the Titan sons of Heaven and Earth,
And failed. They despised cunning; in their pride of strength
They foresaw easy victory and the rule of might.
I knew the appointed course of things to come. My mother,
Themis, or Earth (one person, though of various names),
Had many times foretold to me, that not brute strength,
Not violence, but cunning must give victory
To the rulers of the future. This I explained to them,
With reasons – which they found not worth one moment's
    heed.

Then, of the courses open to me, it seemed best
To take my stand – my mother with me – at the side
Of Zeus, willing and welcome. It was I who gave
That counsel through which ancient Cronos and his crew
Lie buried now in the black abyss of Tartarus.
That was the help I gave the king of the gods; and this
Is my reward – this is his black ingratitude.
To look on all friends with suspicion – this disease
Would seem to be inherent in a tyrant's soul.

Now, for your question, on what charge Zeus tortures me,
I'll tell you. On succeeding to his father's throne
At once he appointed various rights to various gods,
Giving to each his set place and authority.
Of wretched humans he took no account, resolved
To annihilate them and create another race.
This purpose there was no one to oppose but I:
I dared. I saved the human race from being ground
To dust, from total death.

27

For that I am subjected to these bitter pains* —
Agony to endure, heart-rending to behold.
I pitied mortal men; but being myself not thought
To merit pity, am thus cruelly disciplined —
A sight to fix dishonour on the name of Zeus.

CHORUS: Only a heart of iron, a temper carved from rock,
Prometheus, could refuse compassion for your pains.
Had I known, I could have wished never to see this sight;
Now I have seen, sorrow and anger rack my heart.

PROMETHEUS: Indeed my friends feel pity at the sight of me.

CHORUS: Did your offence perhaps go further than you have
said?

PROMETHEUS: Yes: I caused men no longer to foresee their
death.

CHORUS: What cure did you discover for their misery?

PROMETHEUS: I planted firmly in their hearts blind hopeful-
ness.

CHORUS: Your gift brought them great blessing.

PROMETHEUS: I did more than that:
I gave them fire.

CHORUS: What? Men, whose life is but a day,
Possess already the hot radiance of fire?

PROMETHEUS: They do; and with it they shall master many
crafts.

CHORUS: This then was the offence for which you suffer here —

PROMETHEUS: Suffer the unrelenting savagery of Zeus.

CHORUS: And is no end of this ordeal appointed you?

PROMETHEUS: No, none; until such time as he sees fit to
choose.

CHORUS: He never will. What hope is there? Oh, you were
wrong —
Do you not see? To say that you were wrong grieves me,
And tortures you. So let us talk no more of it.
Instead, try now to think of some deliverance.

PROMETHEUS: Oh, it is easy for the one who stands outside

28

The prison-wall of pain to exhort and teach the one
Who suffers. All you have said to me I always knew.
Wrong? I accept the word. I willed, willed to be wrong!
And helping humans I found trouble for myself.
Yet I did not expect such punishment as this —
To be assigned an uninhabited desert peak,
Fastened in mid-air to this crag, and left to rot!

Listen: stop wailing for the pain I suffer now.
Step to the ground; I'll tell you what the future holds
For me; you shall know everything from first to last.
Do what I ask you, do it! Share the suffering
Of one whose turn is now. Grief is a wanderer
Who visits many, bringing always the same gift.

CHORUS: Your appeal falls on willing ears, Prometheus.
Come, sisters, leave your seats
In the ship that flies on the holy highway of birds;
Step lightly down to the rocky ground.
— We are eager to hear to the end
The story of all you have undergone, Prometheus.

> *The* CHORUS *leave their ship. As they group themselves on the
> ground* OCEANUS *arrives seated on a winged four-footed
> creature.*

OCEANUS: Here at last!
Prometheus, I have come a long way to visit you,
Guiding this swift-winged creature
By will, without any bridle.
Believe me, I am sorry for your misfortunes.
Being related to you, I suppose,
Makes me sympathize with you;
But apart from relationship, there is no one
Whom I hold in greater respect.
That is true, and I will prove it to you:
For I am incapable of mere flattery.
Come, now, tell me what I should do to help you.

You shall never say, Prometheus,
That you have any firmer friend than Oceanus.

PROMETHEUS: What's that? Who is it? Ah! So you too have come
To observe my torment? How was it you dared to leave
Your Ocean-river and your rock-roofed natural caves
To visit Earth, mother of iron? Are you here
To gaze at what I suffer, and add your grief to mine?
Behold a spectacle — me here, the friend of Zeus,
By whose help he established his sole sovereignty:
See with what pains I am now disciplined by him.

OCEANUS: I see, Prometheus; and although your mind is subtle
I want at least to give you the best advice I can.
A new king rules among the gods. Then know yourself,
And take upon yourself new ways to suit the time.
If in this way you fling out edged and angry speeches,
It may be Zeus — throned though he is so far above —
Will hear you; and, for result, your present load of troubles
Will seem a childish trifle. Oh, my unhappy friend,
Throw off your angry mood and seek deliverance
From all your suffering. What I say may seem perhaps
Well worn; but your plight is the inescapable
Reward, Prometheus, of a too proud-speaking tongue.
You still will not be humble, will not yield to pain;
You mean to add new sufferings to those you have.
Come now, accept my guidance: we are ruled by one
Whose harsh and sole dominion none may call to account.
Acknowledge this, and cease to kick against the goad.
Now I will go and try if there is any way
Within my power to set you free. Meanwhile, keep quiet,
Don't rage and storm. You are intelligent: full well
You know that punishment falls on the unruly tongue.

PROMETHEUS: I envy you your luck in not being under censure
Even for having dared to sympathize with me.
Now leave it, give it no more thought. Do what you may,

You never will persuade him; he is immovable.
Look out yourself, lest you meet trouble on your way.
OCEANUS: You are a far more prudent counsellor of others
Than of yourself; experience makes this plain to me.
But I'm resolved to go, so say no more against it.
I'm sure – yes, sure that Zeus will grant me what I ask,
And for my sake will loose your bonds and set you free.
PROMETHEUS: I thank you, and shall always thank you. Your
    goodwill
Is all that one could ask. But stir no hand for me;
Your trouble will be wasted, and bring me no good,
Whatever you intend to try. Do nothing, and
Keep clear of danger. If I suffer, I do not therefore
Wish that as many as possible should suffer too;
Far from it. The fate of Atlas grieves me – my own brother,
Who in the far West stands with his unwieldy load
Pressing upon his back, the pillar of heaven and earth.
I pity Typhon, that earth-born destroying giant,
The hundred-headed, native of the Cilician caves;
I saw him, all his fiery strength subdued by force.
Against the united gods he stood, his fearful jaws
Hissing forth terror; from his eyes a ghastly glare
Flashed, threatening to annihilate the throne of Zeus.
But Zeus's sleepless weapon came on him; he felt
The fiery vapour of the crashing thunderbolt,
Which blasted him out of his lofty boasts, and struck
His very heart, and burnt his strength to sulphurous ash.
Now, crushed under Mount Etna's roots, near the sea-strait,
He lies, a helpless sprawling hulk; while on the peak
Hephaestus hammers red-hot iron; and thence one day
Rivers of flame shall burst forth, and with savage jaws
Devour the bright smooth fields of fertile Sicily;
Such rage shall Typhon, though charred with the bolt of Zeus,
Send boiling out in jets of fierce, fire-breathing spume
Unquenchable. But you are not without experience;

31

You have no need of my instruction. Save yourself
As you know how. Meanwhile I'll drink my painful cup
To the dregs, till Zeus relaxes from his angry mood.

OCEANUS: Have you not learnt, Prometheus, anger's a disease
Which words can heal?

PROMETHEUS: Yes, if you soothe the spirit when
The moment's ripe – not roughly baulk a swelling rage.

OCEANUS: Tell me, Prometheus: do you see some risk entailed
Even in my having dared to sympathize with you?

PROMETHEUS: Superfluous labour and light-minded foolishness.

OCEANUS: Let me be guilty then of foolishness. Sometimes
A wise man gains his point by being thought not wise.

PROMETHEUS: In this case it is I who will be thought not wise.

OCEANUS: Your way of speaking plainly sends me home again.

PROMETHEUS: Why, yes. In pitying me I fear you may well gain
An enemy.

OCEANUS: Who? The new-enthroned almighty lord?

PROMETHEUS: Take care; he may turn angry.

OCEANUS: Your fate is a lesson
To me, Prometheus.

PROMETHEUS: Go! Get out! Be what you are!

OCEANUS: I'm anxious to be going; there's no need to shout.
This four-legged beast's already beating with his wings
The smooth path of the air. Yes, he'll be pleased enough
To lie down comfortably in his own stall at home.

Exit OCEANUS.

CHORUS: I weep, Prometheus, for your deadly plight.
Tears flow from my eyes,
Fall in a gentle stream,
And wash my cheek like a spring of water.
In this pitiful sight
Zeus, ruling by laws of his own invention,
Provides an example
Of his proud power over the gods of the past.

Now every country cries aloud in grief:
The peoples of Europe mourn*
For you and the Titan race,
Your glorious, ancient rule and honour;
And all the settled tribes
That graze the fields of holy Asia
Weep loudly for you and share your suffering;

The Amazons of the land of Colchis,
Virgins fearless in battle,
The Scythian hordes who live at the world's end
On the shores of Lake Maeotis;
The warlike princes of Arabia,
Holding their cliff-perched fortress near Mount Caucasus,*
Whose battle-cry strikes terror
In the ranks of sharpened spears, weep for you.

Only once before have I seen
A Titan god so tormented,
Vanquished in bonds invincible;
Atlas, alone in excellence of strength,
Who holds the vault of the sky upon his back, and groans;*

And the wave of the wide Ocean
Roars in unison with him,
The depths of waters weep,
The cavernous darkness of the dead world mutters under,
and the holy fountains of flowing rivers
Weep in pity for his pain.

PROMETHEUS: You must not think it is through pride or
   stubbornness
That I am silent; thought and anger gnaw my heart,
To see myself so outraged. Why, who else but I
Assigned to these new gods their honours, first and last?
All that you know, and I'll not speak of. What I did

For mortals in their misery, hear now. At first
Mindless, I gave them mind and reason. — What I say
Is not in censure of mankind, but showing you
How all my gifts to them were guided by goodwill. —
In those days they had eyes, but sight was meaningless;
Heard sounds, but could not listen; all their length of life
They passed like shapes in dreams, confused and purposeless.
Of brick-built, sun-warmed houses, or of carpentry,
They had no notion; lived in holes, like swarms of ants,
Or deep in sunless caverns; knew no certain way
To mark off winter, or flowery spring, or fruitful summer;
Their every act was without knowledge, till I came.
I taught them to determine when stars rise or set —
A difficult art. Number, the primary science, I
Invented for them, and how to set down words in writing —
The all-remembering skill, mother of many arts.
I was the first to harness beasts under a yoke
With trace or saddle as man's slaves, to take man's place
Under the heaviest burdens; put the horse to the chariot,
Made him obey the rein, and be an ornament
To wealth and greatness. No one before me discovered
The sailor's waggon — flax-winged craft that roam the seas.
Such tools and skills I found for men: myself, poor wretch,
Lack even one trick to free me from this agony.

CHORUS: Humiliation follows pain; distraught in mind
You have lost your way; like a bad doctor fallen ill
You now despair of finding drugs to cure yourself.

PROMETHEUS: Now hear the rest of what I have to tell, what crafts,
What methods I devised — and you will wonder more.
First in importance: if a man fell ill, he had
No remedy, solid or liquid medicine,
Or ointment, but for lack of drugs they pined away;
Until I showed them how to mix mild healing herbs
And so protect themselves against all maladies.

34

Then I distinguished various modes of prophecy,
And was the first to tell from dreams what Fate ordained
Should come about; interpreted the hidden sense
Of voices, sounds, sights met by chance upon the road.
The various flights of crook-clawed vultures I defined
Exactly, those by nature favourable, and those
Sinister; how each species keeps its mode of life;
What feuds, friendships, associations kind with kind
Preserves; how to interpret signs in sacrifice,
Smoothness of heart and lights, what colours please the gods
In each, the mottled shapeliness of liver-lobes.
The thigh-bones wrapped in fat, and the long chine, I burnt,
Leading men on the highway of an occult art;
And signs from flames, obscure before, I now made plain.

So much for prophecy. Next the treasures of the earth,
The bronze, iron, silver, gold hidden deep down – who else
But I can claim to have found them first? No one, unless
He talks like a fool. So, here's the whole truth in one word:
All human skill and science was Prometheus' gift.
CHORUS: Then do not, after helping men to your own hurt,
    Neglect to save yourself from torment. I have hopes
    That you will yet be freed and rival Zeus in power.
PROMETHEUS: Fate fulfils all in time; but it is not ordained
    That these events shall yet reach such an end. My lot
    Is to win freedom only after countless pains.
    Cunning is feebleness beside Necessity.
CHORUS: And whose hand on the helm controls Necessity?
PROMETHEUS: The three Fates; and the Furies, who forget
    nothing.
CHORUS: Has Zeus less power than they?
PROMETHEUS: He cannot fly from Fate.
CHORUS: What fate is given to Zeus, but everlasting power?
PROMETHEUS: This is a thing you may not know; so do not ask.
CHORUS: It is some holy truth you cloak in mystery.

PROMETHEUS: Turn your thoughts elsewhere; now is not the
    time to speak
  Of that; it is a secret which by every means
  Must be kept close. By keeping it I shall escape
  This ignominious prison and these fearful pains.
CHORUS: May Zeus, who disposes all things,
  Never exert his power to crush my will;
  May I never grow weary
  In worshipping the gods with pure offerings of bulls
  Beside the inexhaustible stream of my father Oceanus.
  May I not offend in word; but let this resolve
  Remain unfading in my heart.

  It is a pleasant thing to spend the length of life
  In confidence and hope,
  And to nourish the soul in light and cheerfulness.
  But I shudder when I see you, Prometheus,
  Racked by infinite tortures.
  For you have no fear of Zeus,
  But pursuing your own purpose
  You respect too highly the race of mortals.

  See, my friend, how thankless were all your benefits.
  Tell me, what strength is there, and where,
  What help to be found in men who live for a day?
  Did you not note the helpless infirmity,
  Feeble as a dream,
  Which fetters the blind tribes of men?
  For human purposes shall never trespass
  Outside the harmony of Zeus's government.

  This is the truth I have learnt from your downfall, Prometheus.
  What strikes my ear is the difference
  Between today's sounds of sorrow
  And the songs we sang to grace your marriage,

The song for the bath and the song for the bed,
When you wooed and won with gifts
My sister Hesione for your wedded bride.

Enter Io.

Io: What land is this? What race lives here?
Who is this that I see held in fetters of rock
At the mercy of wind and storm?
For what sin do you suffer such a death?
Tell me, where has my miserable wandering brought me?

　　　[suddenly she shrieks in pain and terror]

The gadfly stings me again. Oh, oh!
I see the ghost of Argus,
The earth-born herdsman with a thousand eyes –
Gods! Keep him away!
He was killed, but no earth can hide him;
He follows me with his crafty gaze;
He escapes from his grave to hound me without mercy,
And drives me starving along the sandy shores;
While the clear music of wax-bound pipes*
Fills my ears with a tune that longs for sleep.

Where, where, where
Will my endless, endless journeys bring me?
Son of Cronos, what have I done?
What sin did you find in me,
To put on me such a yoke of torment,
Plague me to misery and madness
With this driving, stinging terror?
Burn me with fire, let the earth swallow me,
Throw me as food for sea-serpents –
Lord God, will you grudge me this prayer?
I have wandered so far,
I have been punished enough with wandering;
I cannot tell how to escape from pain.
Do you hear my voice? It is Io, the girl with horns!

PROMETHEUS: I hear indeed the frenzied daughter of Inachus
Who fired the heart of Zeus with love, and suffers now
Through Hera's hate her long ordeal of cruel pursuit.
IO: You spoke my father's name: how do you know it?
Tell me who you are – you, as pitiable as I.
You know who I am, and you named truly
The heaven-sent tormentor
Which ravages and drives me with stings.
I have run without rest
In a leaping frenzy of pain and hunger,
The victim of Hera's calculating resentment.
Are there any in all this suffering world
Who endure what I endure?
Tell me clearly what remains for me to suffer,
What resource, what cure can save me.
Speak, if you know; give help and guidance
To the tortured exiled virgin.
PROMETHEUS: I'll tell you plainly everything you wish to learn,
Not weaving mysteries, but in such simple speech
As one should use in speaking to a friend. I am
Prometheus, who bestowed on man the gift of fire.
IO: O universal benefactor of mankind,
Ill-starred Prometheus, why are you thus crucified?
PROMETHEUS: I was lamenting all my pains. I have ceased now.
IO: Will you not tell me –
PROMETHEUS: Ask; I can tell everything.
IO: Who was it, then, that clamped you fast in this ravine?
PROMETHEUS: The will of Zeus decreed; Hephaestus' hand obeyed.
IO: What were the sins for which you suffer punishment?
PROMETHEUS: What I have told you is enough.
IO: Then reveal this:
Where is the end of my cursed wandering, and when?
PROMETHEUS: Not to know this is better for you than to know.

Io: Do not hide from me what it is my doom to suffer.

PROMETHEUS: It is not that I grudge you what you ask of me.

Io: Why then do you hesitate to tell me the whole truth?

PROMETHEUS: Not from ill will. I shrink from shattering your
    heart.

Io: Come, do not take more thought for me than I would wish.

PROMETHEUS: Since you're determined, I must tell you.
    Listen then.

CHORUS: Not yet. Let us too share this pleasure. Let us ask
    Io to tell us first the story of her affliction,
    And hear the ruin of her life from her own lips.
    Then let her learn from you what she must yet endure.

PROMETHEUS: It is for you, Io, to grant them their request;
    And more especially, since they are your father's sisters.
    Tears and lamenting find their due reward when those
    Who listen are ready too with tears of sympathy.

Io: I cannot disobey; you shall hear everything
    You want to know, in plain words; though even to speak
    Of those events from which my troubles first arose,
    And my unhappy transformation, makes me weep.

        At night in my own room visions would visit me,
    Repeating in seductive words, 'Most blessed maid,
    Why live a virgin for so long? Love waits for you –
    The greatest: Zeus, inflamed with arrows of desire,
    Longs to unite with you in love. Do not reject,
    My child, the bed of Zeus. Go out to the deep grass
    Of Lerna, where your father's sheep and cattle graze,
    That the eye of Zeus may rest from longing and be satisfied'.

        By such dreams every troubled night I was beset,
    Until I dared to tell my father. Then he sent
    Messengers many times to Pytho and Dodona
    To learn what he must do or say to please the gods.
    They came back with reports of riddling oracles,

Obscurely worded, hard to interpret. But at last
Was given a clear utterance unmistakably
Commanding Inachus to turn me from his house
And city, to wander homeless* to the ends of the earth;
If he refused, the fiery thunderbolt of Zeus
Would fall and extirpate his race to the last man.

Such was the oracle of Loxias. My father
Yielded, and sent me forth, and locked his door against me –
He as unwilling as myself; but he was forced
To do this by the cruel bridle-rein of Zeus.
At once my shape was changed, my mind distorted. Horned,
As you now see, stung by the gadfly's stabbing goad,
Convulsed and mad, I rushed on, to the crystal stream
Of Cerchnea and the spring of Lerna; I was followed
By Argus, a giant herdsman of ungoverned rage,
Who watched my every step with his ten thousand eyes.
A sudden, unexpected stroke robbed him of life.
I, gadfly-maddened, still am driven from land to land,
Lashed by this God-appointed scourge.

                                        That is my story.
If you can say what still remains to be endured,
Tell me; and do not out of pity comfort me
With lies. I count false words the foulest plague of all.

CHORUS: What a pitiful, terrible fate!
Never did I dream that so strange a story
Would ever come to my ears;
That anguish, cruelty, terror,
So bitter to see and to endure,
Would ever chill my spirit with a wound so sharp.
Alas, Fate, Fate!
I see the lot of Io, and tremble.

PROMETHEUS: You shed your tears too early, like a frightened
        woman.
Keep them until you hear what is to follow now.

40

CHORUS: Speak, then, and tell her all. It comforts those in pain
　To know beforehand all the pain they still must bear.
PROMETHEUS: Your first request to me was easily obtained;
　You wished to hear Io's ordeal from her own lips.
　Now hear the rest – what sufferings at Hera's hands
　Are yet in store for this young maid. Now lay to heart
　My words, daughter of Inachus, and learn the goal
　Of all your journeys.

　　From this place turn first toward the rising sun, and pass
　Over the unploughed plains until you reach the land
　Of nomad Scythians, living high above the ground
　In houses built on strong-wheeled carts, with wattled roofs.
　They are armed with powerful bows; keep well away from them,
　And take your path by the loud-roaring rocky shore,
　And so pass through that country. Next, on your left hand,
　Is the country of the Chalybes, craftsmen in iron.
　Beware of them; they are savage, and no stranger can
　Approach them safely. After this you reach the river
　Hybristes, whose wild torrent justifies its name.
　Do not attempt to cross – it is too dangerous –
　Until you come to Caucasus itself, the peak
　Of all that range, where from the very brows the river
　Floods forth its fury. You must cross the topmost ridge
　Close to the stars, and take the pathway leading south.
　There you will find the warlike race of Amazons,
　Haters of men. This race in time to come shall found
　The city of Themiscyra, on the Thermodon,
　Where the rough jaw of Salmydessus fronts the sea,
　An enemy to sailors, stepmother to ships.
　The Amazons will most gladly guide you on your way.
　Next, where a narrow creek gives entrance to a lake,
　You will come to the Cimmerian Isthmus. Boldly then

Leave land, and cross the Maeotic Strait. Ages to come
Shall tell the story of your passage, and the place
Shall be called Bosporus to commemorate you. Thus
From Europe you will reach the Asian continent.

       Does it not seem to you that this king of the gods
In all matters alike is given to violence?
A god, lusting for union with this mortal maid,
He dooms her to such journeys! You are unfortunate,
Io, in your lover. All that I have told so far
Hardly begins – believe me! – all there is to tell.

Io [*weeping*]: Oh, oh! I cannot bear it!

PROMETHEUS: More cries and groans? When you shall hear
    the rest, what then?

CHORUS: Have you still more to tell her of distress and pain?

PROMETHEUS: I have, a stormy sea of deadly misery.

Io: Why should I go on living? Why not hurl myself
    At once down from this rocky cliff, be dashed in pieces,
    And find relief from all my pain? Better to die
    Once, than to suffer torment all my living days.

PROMETHEUS: Then you would find it hard to bear *my* agonies,
    Since I am fated not to die. Death would have brought
    Release; but now no end to suffering is in sight
    For me, until Zeus be deposed from sovereignty.

Io: What? Is it possible that Zeus should be deposed?

PROMETHEUS: You would be glad, I think, to see that come
    about.

Io: How could I help it, after all he has made me suffer?

PROMETHEUS: Learn it as truth: it shall be so.

Io: By whom shall Zeus
    Be stripped of power?

PROMETHEUS: By his own foolish purposes.

Io: How will it happen? Tell me, if it does no harm.

PROMETHEUS: He plans a union that will turn to his undoing.

Io: With mortal or immortal? Tell me, if you may.

PROMETHEUS: Why ask with whom? That is a thing I may not tell.

IO: Then is it she who will unseat him from his throne?

PROMETHEUS: She is to bear a son more powerful than his father.

IO: Is there no way by which Zeus can escape this fate?

PROMETHEUS: None, but with my help. I could save him, once set free.

IO: But if Zeus be unwilling, who can set you free?

PROMETHEUS: A child of yours is named as my deliverer.

IO: What do you say? My child shall free you from these chains?

PROMETHEUS: Yes, in the thirteenth generation after you.

IO: I find it hard to interpret this last prophecy.

PROMETHEUS: Then do not seek to learn your own appointed lot.

IO: You offered me this favour; do not now refuse.

PROMETHEUS: I'll grant you one or other of two prophecies.

IO: What are they? Offer me my choice.

PROMETHEUS: Then choose between
The remainder of your journey, and my deliverer.

CHORUS: Of these two favours, if you please, grant one to her,
And one to me, Prometheus; do not grudge the telling.
Reveal to Io all her future wandering,
And tell me who shall set you free. I long to know.

PROMETHEUS: Since you are eager, I will not refuse to tell
Everything you desire. First, Io, I will name
The many lands where Fate will toss you in your journey;
Write what I tell you in your book of memory.

When you have crossed the stream that bounds two continents
Press on, over the surge of the sea, towards the east
Where the sun stalks in flame, to the Gorgonean land,
Cisthene. There live Phorcys' aged virgin daughters,
In shape like swans, possessing one eye and one tooth

43

Between the three; beings on whom no ray of sun
Ever looks down, nor moon at night. And close to them
Their three winged sisters, loathed enemies of humankind,
The snake-haired Gorgons, whom no man can see and live.
This is but the beginning. Now hear yet another
Grim sight you must encounter: beware the silent hounds
Of Zeus, the sharp-beaked griffins; and beware the tribe
Of one-eyed Arimaspian horsemen, on the banks
Of the Plutonian river whose waters wash down gold.
Do not go near them. Then you will reach a remote region
Where near the sun's bright fountains live a dark-skinned race.
There is the Ethiopian river; follow its course
Down, till you reach the cataract where from the Bybline hills
The Nile pours forth his holy stream to quench men's thirst.
And he will guide you to the delta of the Nile
Where, Io, you and your descendants shall at last
By Fate's appointment found your far-off colony.

If any point is indistinct or hard to follow
Ask further, and make sure that you have understood.
I have more time to spare than I would wish to have.
CHORUS: If anything passed over still remains to tell
Of Io's painful journeys, speak. If not, grant now
To us the favour which, you remember, we asked of you.
PROMETHEUS: Io has heard the whole course of her wandering.
And, lest she think I may have given her idle words,
I'll speak of what she suffered before coming here,
To prove my words. Most of the details I'll omit,
And come directly to your recent wanderings.

On reaching the Molossian plains, and the rock-wall
Which towers above Dodona, where Thesprotian Zeus
Has his oracular seat, where grow the speaking oaks –
A marvel past belief – by which you were addressed
Plainly and unambiguously as the destined bride

Of Zeus – does that truth touch you? – from that place you
   rushed,
Plagued by the gadfly's sting, along the sea-shore path
To the wide Adriatic,* whence back yet again
The storm of frenzy drove you on your wild flight here.
And that bay of the sea shall for all future time –
Mark this – be called Ionian, to perpetuate
For all mankind the story of Io's wanderings.
I tell you this as proof that my prophetic mind
Sees more than meets the eye. Now to you all I'll tell
The rest, resuming at the point where I broke off.

   Where the Nile's outflow lays its bank of silt, there
   stands
On the last edge of land the city of Canopus;
And here at last Zeus shall restore your mind, and come
Upon you, not with terror, with a gentle touch;
His hand laid on you shall put life into your womb,
And you shall bear a dark-skinned son to Zeus, and name him
From his begetting, 'Child of a touch', Epaphos.
He shall possess the harvest-wealth of all those lands
Watered by the broad-flowing Nile. Five generations
From him, a family of fifty sisters shall return
Against their will to Argos, desperate to escape
From kindred marriage with their cousins. The young men
Follow in passionate pursuit close on their track,
As hawks hunt doves; lusting for an unlawful love.*
But God shall grudge them the enjoyment of their brides.
And Argive soil shall welcome them, when in the night
Bold resolution goes on guard, and women's hands
Make war and slaughter, and male pride is overthrown.
For each shall plunge her sharp sword in his throat, and kill
Her husband. May such love come to my enemies!
But sweet desire shall charm one girl, and blunt the edge
Of her resolve, and she shall spare her husband's life,

And choose to be called coward, but not murderess;
And she shall live in Argos and give birth to kings.

And from her children's children shall be born in time
(To trace each step would take too long) a fearless hero
Famed as an archer, who shall free me from these bonds.
Such is the oracle as my mother told it me,
Titanian Themis, born in the old time. But how
All this shall come about, would take me long to tell,
And you in listening would gain nothing.

                     I o *interrupts with a wild cry of pain.*

Io: The stroke of madness burns me again,
    My brain is convulsed, the gadfly
    Stings me with his immortal arrow.
    My heart beats wildly in my body;
    My eyeballs roll and turn;
    Insanity falls on me like a raging storm
    And drives me off course;
    I can't govern my tongue; words rush out at random,
    Beating against waves of deadly ruin!*

                     Exit I o.

Chorus: He was a wise man indeed
    Who first weighed this thought in his mind
    And gave it utterance in speech,
    That the best rule by far
    Is to marry in your own rank;
    That a man who works with his hands should never crave
    To marry either a woman pampered by wealth
    Or one who prides herself on her noble family.

    O Fates, who bring all things to fulfilment,
    May you never see me sharing the bed of Zeus;
    May I never be joined in marriage with any god!
    For I tremble when I look at the girlhood of Io,
    Denied the love of a man,

Tormented in ever-restless exile
By the cruelty of Hera.

When marriage is with an equal
For me it holds no fear or danger.
But may the love of the greater gods
Never cast on me its irresistible glance.
That is a fight which cannot be fought,
The straight road to despair.
What would become of me I cannot say;
For I see no way to escape the design of Zeus.

PROMETHEUS: I swear that Zeus, for all his obstinacy, shall yet
Be humbled, so disastrous shall this marriage prove
Which he proposes – a marriage that shall hurl him out
Of throne and sovereignty into oblivion.
And then the curse his father Cronos cursed him with,
The day he lost his ancient throne, shall all come true.
There is no god but I who can reveal to him
The way to avert this ignominy. I know it all.
So now let him sit on, serenely confident
In his celestial thunders, brandishing in his hand
His fierce fire-breathing thunderbolt – that will not save him:
His fall will be sure, shameful, unendurable!
Such an antagonist he is even now himself
Preparing against himself, a wonder irresistible,
One who will find a flame hotter than lightning-strokes,
A crash to overwhelm the thunder; one whose strength
Shall split Poseidon's trident-spear, that dreaded scourge
That shakes both sea and land. This is the reef on which
His power shall strike and founder, till he learns how great
A chasm lies between ruling and being ruled.

CHORUS: These threats against Zeus surely voice but your own
wish.

PROMETHEUS: I speak what shall prove true – and my own
wish as well.

CHORUS: Must we expect one who shall bring Zeus to his
    knees?

PROMETHEUS: Yes; Zeus's neck shall bow beneath worse
    pains than mine.

CHORUS: Why are you not afraid to fling such taunting words?

PROMETHEUS: Why should I fear? My destiny is not to
    die.

CHORUS: Zeus might invent for you some still worse agony.

PROMETHEUS: Then let him do it! I am prepared for every-
    thing.

CHORUS: A wise man will speak humbly, and fear Nemesis.*

PROMETHEUS: Bow! Pray! As always, fawn upon the powerful
    hand!
  For great Zeus I care less than nothing. Let him do
  And govern as he wills, for the short time he has.
  He will not govern long among the gods. – Why, look!
  Here comes his runner, the new tyrant's lickspittle.
  No doubt he brings some message.

Enter HERMES.

HERMES: I speak to you – the master-mind, with heart more
    sour
  Than sourness; you who honoured creatures of a day
  And sinned against immortals; you, the thief of fire:
  The Father bids you tell him what this marriage is
  Through which you boast that he shall fall from power. Now
    speak
  No clever riddles, but set forth the detailed truth.
  Do not, Prometheus, make me travel all this way
  Again; Zeus is not mollified by such replies.

PROMETHEUS: This underling of gods makes a high-sounding
    speech
  Crammed with importance. – You and all your crew are
    young;
  So is your power; and you imagine that you hold
  An unassailable citadel. But I have seen

48

Two dynasties already hurled from those same heights;
And I shall see the third, today's king, fall to earth
More shamefully than his precursors, and more soon.
Do you think I quake and cower before these upstart gods?
Not much, nor little – not one slightest thought! Now you
Trot back the way you came; you'll find out nothing here.

HERMES: Conduct like this, both obstinate and insolent,
Has once already brought you to a painful plight.

PROMETHEUS: Understand this: I would not change my painful plight,
On any terms, for your servile humility.

HERMES: Being bondslave to this rock is preferable, no doubt,
To being the trusted messenger of Father Zeus.

PROMETHEUS: You use the fitting language of the insolent.

HERMES: It seems you find your present state a luxury.

PROMETHEUS: You think so? May I one day see my enemies,
And you among them, in such luxury as this!

HERMES: What, I? Do you blame me too for your sufferings?

PROMETHEUS: In one word, I detest all gods who could repay
My benefits with such outrageous infamy.

HERMES: It's plain that your insanity is far advanced.

PROMETHEUS: Perhaps – if to hate enemies is insanity.

HERMES: Now you, free and in power, would be unbearable.

PROMETHEUS: Alas!

HERMES: Alas? That word is one which Zeus has never known.

PROMETHEUS: But Time, as he grows older, teaches everything.

HERMES: Time has not taught *you* self-control or prudence – yet.

PROMETHEUS: No – or I would not argue with an underling.

HERMES: It seems you'll tell nothing of what Zeus wants to know.

PROMETHEUS: And yet I owe him much – that I would gladly pay.

HERMES: You banter with me – do you think I am a child?

49

PROMETHEUS: Are you not then a child, or worse than child-
　　ish, if
　　You still expect to get an answer out of me?
　　There is no torture, no ingenuity, by which
　　Zeus can persuade me to reveal my secret, till
　　The injury of these bonds is loosed from me. Therefore
　　Let scorching flames be flung from heaven; let the whole earth
　　With white-winged snowstorms, subterranean thunderings,
　　Heave and convulse: nothing will force me to reveal
　　By whose hand Fate shall hurl Zeus from his tyranny.
HERMES: Consider now whether this course seems profitable.
PROMETHEUS: I have long ago considered all this, and re-
　　solved.
HERMES: Come, bring yourself, perverse fool, while there is
　　still time,
　　To weigh your situation, and so turn to sense.
PROMETHEUS: You waste your breath; you may as well exhort
　　the waves.
　　Never persuade yourself that I, through fear of what
　　Zeus may intend, will show a woman's mind, or kneel
　　To my detested enemy, with womanish hands
　　Outspread in supplication for release. No, never!
HERMES: My words lead only to more words, without effect;
　　Beg as I may, nothing can soothe or soften you.
　　Like an unbroken colt you try your strength, and take
　　The bit between your teeth, and fight against the reins.
　　Yet all your violence springs from feeble reckoning;
　　For obstinacy in a fool has by itself
　　No strength at all. Consider now what punishments
　　Will burst inevitably upon you like a storm
　　Of mountainous waves, if you refuse to listen to me.

　　　First, Zeus will split this rugged chasm with the shock
　　And flame of lightning, and entomb you underground
　　Still clamped on this embracing rock. When a long age

Has passed, you will return into the light; and then
The dark-winged hound of Zeus will come, the savage eagle,
An uninvited banqueter, and all day long
Will rip your flesh in rags and feast upon your liver,
Gnawing it black. And you may hope for no release
From such a torment, till some god be found* to take
Your pains upon him, and of his own will descend
To sunless Hades and the black depths of Tartarus.

So think again; this is no fabricated boast,
But truth as Zeus has spoken it, who cannot lie,
But will accomplish every word his mouth has uttered.
Look every way; consider; and be sure of this:
Wise counsel always is worth more than stubbornness.
CHORUS: To us it seems that Hermes' words are sensible.
He bids you quit resistance and seek good advice.
Do so; a wise man's folly forfeits dignity.
PROMETHEUS: I knew what Hermes had to say
Before he made his brag. It is no dishonour
For an enemy to suffer at his enemy's hands.
So let the pronged locks of lightning be launched at me,
Let the air be roused with thunder and convulsion of wild
    winds,
Let hurricanes upheave by the roots the base of the earth,
Let the sea-waves' roaring savagery
Confound the courses of the heavenly stars;
Let him lift me high and hurl me to black Tartarus
On ruthless floods of irresistible doom:
I am one whom he cannot kill.
HERMES: Thoughts and words like these
Are what one may hear from lunatics.
This prayer of his shows all the features of frenzy;
And I see no sign of improvement.
[to the CHORUS] You, however, who sympathize with his
    sufferings,

Get away quickly from this place,
Lest the intolerable roar of thunder stun your senses.

CHORUS: If you want to persuade me, use a different tone
And give other advice. You speak too hastily,
Bidding me do what I could not think of doing.
Would you have me practise cowardice?
I will stay with Prometheus, come what must.
I was taught to hate those who desert their friends;
And there is no infamy I more despise.

HERMES: Then remember my warning;
And when you are caught by calamity
Don't lay the blame on Fortune, or say that Zeus
Plunged you in suffering unforeseen;
Not Zeus but yourselves will be to blame.
You know what is coming; it is neither sudden nor secret.
Only your own folly will entangle you
In the inextricable net of destruction.

Exit HERMES.

PROMETHEUS: Now it is happening: threat gives place to performance.
The earth rocks; thunder, echoing from the depth,
Roars in answer; fiery lightnings twist and flash.
Dust dances in a whirling fountain;
Blasts of the four winds skirmish together,
Set themselves in array for battle;
Sky and sea rage indistinguishably.
The cataclysm advances visibly upon me,
Sent by Zeus to make me afraid.

O Earth, my holy mother,
O sky, where sun and moon
Give light to all in turn,
You see how I am wronged!

The rock collapses and disappears, as the
CHORUS *scatter in all directions.*

THE SUPPLIANTS

THE SUPPLIANTS

*

CHORUS *of the fifty daughters of Danaus*
DANAUS, *a descendant of Zeus and Io*
PELASGUS, *King of Argos*
HERALD *of the Egyptians*
SECOND CHORUS *of Maids attending the Danaids*
Other Soldiers and Attendants

*

Near the coast of the Peloponnese; a meadow with a grassy mound on which stand a number of altars and images of gods, including Zeus, Apollo, Poseidon and Hermes. In the distant background the walls and towers of Argos can be seen. The daughters of Danaus are grouped near the images.

CHORUS: May Zeus, the suppliants' god, look kindly on us all.
   We have come by ship from the powdered dunes
   At the outer mouth of the River Nile;
   The land we have left is dear to Zeus,
   Sharing the Syrian pastures; yet we come
   Not under ban for guilt of blood,
   Not driven out by a city's sentence:
   Exile is our choice,
   Our hope of escape from lust of men,
   From abhorred and impious union with Aegyptus' sons.

   Danaus our father leads our cause
   And guides us in each resolute move.
   His choice of evils judged it best
   To flock for safety over the sea

To the land of Argos. Here it was
Our race began, which, now full-grown,
Claims origin from that tormented beast,
Quickened with the touch and breath of Zeus himself.

To what land kinder than Argos could we come,
Armed with these, the suppliant's weapons,
Branches decked with wool?
O city! Soil of this land, and gleaming waters!
Gods of the air, spirits inhabiting
Dark chambers of earth, honoured with sombre rites!
And, third in my prayer, Zeus, Saviour,
Whose hand guides the helm of the upright,
Receive this company of suppliant women;
Let pity greet us from Argos like a gentle wind!

But the male pride of the violent sons of Aegyptus —
Before they ever tread this marshy coast,
Hurl, together with their pursuing vessel,
Out to the open sea! There, met
By the fierce buffeting storm,
By thunder, lightning, wind, and rain of the wild ocean,
Let them die, before ever they lay hands
On us their cousins, to enter our unwilling beds,
Which Right forbids them!

Now from across the sea
I invoke as our protector
The child pastured amid flowers,
The Calf whom Zeus begot*
Of the Cow, mother of our race,
Made pregnant by the breathing and caress of Zeus;
Thence his true name was given,
His life fulfilled as it was foretold,
When his mother bore Epaphos, 'Child of a touch'.

Him now I invoke
Here in the fields which pastured
Io, our prime mother;
Now I, recounting what was suffered then,
Will give clear proof of what we claim today;
And other like proofs soon,
Although unlooked-for, shall appear;
For as time lengthens truth is known.

If any native of this shore
By chance is near, listening to the cries of birds,
He will think, when our sad suppliant chant
Falls on his ear, that he is hearing
The voice of Tereus' wife, the tearful Daulian,
The nightingale hawk-hunted,
Who weeping under green foliage
Grieves for her life exiled from home,
And tells in song the manner of her son's death;
How by her own hand, a prey
To his mother's fierce passion, he perished.

So I, moved to lament in Ionian dirges,
Ravage with grief the softness
Of cheeks the Nile has ripened,*
And a heart unskilled in tears.
I pluck the flowers of anguish,
Grazing my flock of terrors.
Will any come to help us,
Fugitives from a land so far away?

Hear us, you gods of marriage: let Justice triumph;
Let wild youth not accomplish
Its wicked lust; let pride
Be quelled by your abhorrence;
Fulfil for us such wedlock as is right.

Even for those who fly the trampling of battle
There is an altar of refuge from destruction,
Where reverence for the gods will keep them safe.

It has been truly said,
'The strong desire of Zeus is hard to hunt.'*
For him all things shine clear,
Though he hide them in black darkness
From the eyes of men that perish.
When by the nod of Zeus
It is decreed that a thing be accomplished,
The event falls firm on its feet.
For the paths of his purposing heart
Stretch dark and tangled, baffling sight and thought.

From their high-towering hopes
He hurls mortals to their destruction;
And there is no immortal
Who unsheathes against him the effortless power of godhead,
But Zeus in a moment punishes his pride,
Though throned in the worship of men.
So let Zeus look on human arrogance, and mark
How lusting for our flesh makes an old stock grow young,
Bloom with perverse desire,
While crazed resolve goads without respite,
And mischief pursuing illusion is pursued by pain.

Chanting such songs, unskilled and unmelodious,
My tearful voice now shrill, now deep,
Songs full of wailing like a ritual dirge,
With living groans I solemnize my death.
I cry for mercy to these Apian* highlands
(Forgive, soil of Hellas, my outlandish tongue);
And again, again I tear
My Tyrian veil* to unsightly rags.

When all goes well, when death no longer threatens,
Then flows forth payment of vows to the gods.
But I am perplexed with danger and difficulty.
Where will this storm lead me?
I cry for mercy to these Apian highlands
(Forgive, soil of Hellas, my outlandish tongue);
And again, again I tear
My Tyrian veil to unsightly rags.

So far the oars of our ship
And the hull sewn with wax to keep out the sea
Have brought us with a fair wind;
No storm has hurt us, and I am thankful.
Now the end of our journey is on land;
May Zeus the all-seeing Father guide it as we desire,
And grant that we, descendants of Io his holy bride,
May escape the embrace of man,
And keep our virginity unconquered.

And may Artemis, daughter of Zeus, lover of chastity,
Who foiled Orion's lust for Opis,
In mercy respect my chaste desires;
Let her come in all her strength,
A virgin to a virgin's rescue,
And foil this lust that pursues us;
That we, descendants of Io the bride of Zeus,
May escape the embrace of man,
And keep our virginity unconquered.

And if not – then to the house the sun abhors,
To Zeus of the lower earth, lord of the dead,
Who welcomes guests without number,
We will come with our suppliant branches;
For we will hang and die by the noose,
If the gods of Olympus refuse to hear us.

Anger of gods, alas,
Searches you out, Io, for punishment;
I know the wedded jealousy of the heavenly ones;
From a wind that blows in anger a storm will follow.

And then Zeus will be found with no just defence,
When, having first slighted
The son of the Cow, whom he himself begot,
He now from that son's offspring averts his eyes,
When we pray to him;
For he hears our cry clearly, however high he sits.

Anger of gods, alas,
Is searching you out, Io, for punishment;
I know the wedded jealousy of the heavenly ones:
From a wind that blows in anger a storm will follow.

> *Meanwhile* DANAUS *has entered from the shore.*

DANAUS: Children, we must be wise. While sailing here you
    found
Your father a wise captain, old and trustworthy;
And now on land I will take careful thought for you
And guard you; only, keep what I say written in your hearts.

> [*he looks and points towards Argos*]

I see dust rise, which without voice proclaims an army
Whose rattling wheels and axles are not yet heard; I see
A mass of men with shields and spears; their horses too,
And their curved chariots. This country's rulers, without
    doubt,
Told of our landing, come to see us for themselves.
Whether this fierce approach be harmless in intent,
Or edged with savage anger, in either case, my daughters,
You had best sit as suppliants to these festal gods*
Here on this mound. An altar is stronger than a fortress,
An impenetrable shield. Come, come quickly; bring your
    branches

Decked with white wool, symbols of Zeus the merciful,
Holding them ceremoniously in your left hands;
Answer these men of Argos as newcomers should,
With words to move tears and compassion for your need;
Say clearly why you have fled here, and that your hands
Are innocent of blood. And mind this above all:
No boldness, and no looseness, in your speech or looks;
A lowly, modest bearing and a steadfast eye.
Be neither forward nor reluctant in your speech.
This is a hasty-tempered race. Remember, then —
Submit! You all are aliens, helpless fugitives;
And for the weaker side bold speech is out of place.

CHORUS: Father, we are wise enough to welcome your wise
    warning.
  And Zeus be witness to us, author of our race!

DANAUS: Then waste no time, but make your sanctuary sure.

CHORUS: I am ready; let me take my seat here at your side.
  O Zeus, have pity on our plight; let us not die!

DANAUS: May Zeus indeed look on us with a friendly eye.
  If Zeus be for us, all will have a happy end.
  Here is Apollo, son of Zeus; now call on him.

CHORUS: We call on the sun's saving beams, and on Apollo
  Holy and pure — and banished once, a god, from heaven:
  He will respect in mortals the misery he knew.

DANAUS: Amen! May he stand by us, championing our cause!

CHORUS: Which other of these gods shall I now call upon?

DANAUS: Look: here I see the trident of the Isthmian god.*

CHORUS: He blessed our voyage; now may he welcome us on
  land.

DANAUS: And here, again, is Hermes, in his Grecian form.

CHORUS: He is well met; now may he herald us good fortune.

DANAUS: In short, name all the gods whom this one altar
    honours;
  And like a flock of doves that cower in fear of hawks
  Claim sanctuary from kindred who are enemies

And would pollute your race. Could bird eat flesh of bird
And yet be pure? And can a man mate with a woman
Against her and her father's will, and yet be pure?
Even after death, in Hades, such an act can never
Escape sentence; there too, they say, among the dead
Another Zeus holds a last judgement on men's crimes.
Be prudent then; answer the leader of these men
So that your enterprise may win success today.

    KING PELASGUS *has now entered with a bodyguard.*

KING: We greet you. From what country do you come? Your
    clothes
Are strange to us – close-woven, soft, barbaric gowns
Such as no woman of Argos or of Hellas wears.
And how you dared to come thus fearless to our shores
Unheralded, unsponsored, without friend or guide,
Is cause for wonder. Branches, indeed, the suppliant's badge,
Lie by your sides before these gods of festival.
This sign alone we can interpret; for the rest,
Conjecture well might breed conjecture endlessly
Were there no voice to answer with the certain truth.

CHORUS: Sir, from our clothing you have guessed the truth.
    And you –
Are you a citizen? Or should I speak to you
As to an invested envoy* – or this city's king?

KING: Speak to me with all confidence. I am Pelasgus,
Son of earth-born Palaechthon, and ruler of this land.
The race that cultivates this soil is fitly named
Pelasgian, after me their king; and all the country
Westward, through which the Haliacmon flows, I rule.
I mark as mine all the Perrhaebian territory,
The lands beyond Mount Pindus, near the Chaones,
And the Dodonian range; only where land meets sea
My empire ends: all between there and here I rule.
The Apian land itself, this level plain, was named
From Apis, known in old times for his healing skill.

A son of Apollo, master of cures and divinations,
He crossed the water from Naupactus, and cleansed this land
From beasts that prey on men – creatures whom Earth, defiled
By guilt of ancient murders, like a cruel stepmother
Brought forth – fierce serpent-swarms to share man's heritage.
For these plagues Apis practised remedies of drugs
And cleansing rituals; and our land was well content,
And for reward now names him in her days of prayer.

I have spoken. Now let one of you declare your race,
And clearly, in few words. Argos dislikes long speech.
CHORUS: Then, in few words, and clearly: we claim Argive
    blood.
The cow whom Zeus made fertile – we are of her breed.
Listen: my words shall weld a proof of all I've said.
KING: Women, I find your story incredible. How can
A race like yours be Argive?* You resemble rather
Libyans – certainly not women of our country.
The Nile might foster such a plant; and in your faces,
Where the male craftsman moulds the female feature, there,
Stamped to the life, is Cyprus; and I hear there are
Women such as you, Nomads, who mount on camels' backs
As we on horses, and ride at ease about the land
That neighbours Ethiopia; if you were armed with bows
I would have guessed you were those famous Amazons,
Who live without men and feed on flesh. But tell me clearly
How you derive from Argos your descent and blood.
CHORUS: Is there a story told that here in Argos once
Io was keeper of the keys of Hera's temple?
KING: That she was, certainly; the story is well known.
CHORUS: And do they add that Zeus was stung with love for
    her?
KING: Yes; and his love was known to Hera's jealousy.
CHORUS: What was the outcome of this royal feud?
KING: A cow

That was a woman, whom the Argive goddess changed.

CHORUS: And Zeus — was he not drawn to seek her?

KING: So they say,
Taking upon him, suitably, the form of a bull.

CHORUS: And what did Hera then — determined as she is?

KING: Set an all-seeing guard to keep watch on the cow.

CHORUS: And who was this all-seeing herdsman of one beast?

KING: Argus, offspring of Earth, whom Hermes killed.

CHORUS: What else
Did Hera then devise against the ill-fated cow?

KING: A fly that torments cattle and will not let them rest.

CHORUS: Yes — known as Oestrus among people of the Nile.

KING: What? Did he drive her even as far as to the Nile?

CHORUS: Yes. All your answers fit my purpose in questioning.

KING: Then to Canopus — even to Memphis did she come?

CHORUS: Yes. There Zeus touched her with his hand, and
begot his child.

KING: What man, then, claims to be the calf of Zeus's cow?

CHORUS: Epaphos, truly named from Zeus's claiming touch.

KING: And what children were born to Epaphos?

CHORUS: A daughter,
Libya, who reaps the harvests of earth's largest land.

KING: What child had she, whom you have yet to name?

CHORUS: Belus,
Who had two sons, and was father to my father here.

KING: Tell me, how do you name his wisdom?

CHORUS: Danaus;
He has a brother also who has fifty sons.

KING: Then do not grudge to tell me his name too.

CHORUS: Aegyptus.
And since you now know the long story of our race,
I beg you, act as champion of this Argive band.

KING: Certainly it seems that you belong from earliest days
To Argos. But how had you heart and will to leave
Your father's home? What stroke of fortune fell on you?

CHORUS: King of the Pelasgians, human ills wear many
colours;
On trouble's wing you will not find two plumes alike.
Who ever thought to take this sudden flight, to sail
To Argos, bound to us by ancient ties of blood,
Driven by loathing of unholy rape in Egypt?

KING: As suppliants of these gods, bearing fresh-gathered
boughs
Decked with white wool, what favour do you ask of me?

CHORUS: That we may not be chattels of Aegyptus' sons.

KING: Why? Do you hate them? Or hold it wrong to marry
them?

CHORUS: What girl would buy a master of her own family?*

KING: Marriage within the family gives increase of strength.

CHORUS: Yes; and if trouble comes, divorce is all too easy.

KING: How then shall I honour your suppliant claim on me?

CHORUS: When they demand us, then refuse to give us up.

KING: And undertake a dangerous war? It is much to ask.

CHORUS: Justice will champion those who fight for her.

KING: Ah, true –
Had I been party to this cause from the beginning.

CHORUS: Respect these gods, your city's helm, thus garlanded.

KING: I see this holy place shady with boughs, and tremble.

CHORUS: Zeus, the suppliant's god, is terrible in anger.
Son of Palaechthon, King of the Pelasgians,
Listen to me with a friendly heart;
Look upon me, a suppliant exile,
Running this way and that
Like a heifer chased by a wolf over the steep rocks,
Where, trusting in the herdsman's help,
She bellows to tell him of her sufferings.

KING: I see the whole company of these festival gods
Nodding assent beneath their shade of fresh-plucked leaves.
Since blood unites you with our city, may your cause
Bring us no harm; no war from any hidden source

Break on us unprepared; that is not what we seek.

CHORUS: May Themis, friend of suppliants, daughter
Of Zeus who gives to each his due,
See that our flight be harmless.
Old in knowledge, learn from the later born:
If you respect the suppliant,
The sacrifice you pay will be the best
That a man of pure life can offer
On the gracious altars of the gods.*

KING: It is not *my* house at whose hearth you sit; and if
The Argive State stands liable to guilt herein,*
The people of Argos must together work its cure.
Therefore I'll undertake no pledge till I have shared
This issue in full council with my citizens.

CHORUS: *You* are the State,* *you* are the people.
Ruler unquestioned, you control
The altar that is your country's hearth;
You fear no vote; by your mere nod
You, monarch on one throne, decide all issues:
Therefore, guard against guilt.

KING: Guilt fall upon my enemies. Yet I do not know
How without harm I can assist you; and again,
To ignore such an appeal shows an ungracious heart.
What can I do? Where turn? I fear either to act,
Or not to act, and so let events take their own course.

CHORUS: Beware the watchful eye of Heaven
That looks on mortal grief, and sees
When men in vain sit at their neighbour's hearth,
Denied their lawful just redress.
The anger of Zeus for a suppliant scorned
Remains, and is not softened
By tears of the man on whom it falls.

KING: If by your country's laws the sons of Aegyptus *are*
Your masters, since they claim to be your next of kin,
Who could oppose their plea? By your own laws you must

65

Be tried, and prove these men have no right over you.

CHORUS: Right or no right, I will not be
Man's chattel won by violence.
I'll stretch my flight from this cruel arrogant rape
Far as the stars stretch over earth.
Choose Justice then for your ally, and give
That holy judgement the gods approve.

KING: To judge is no easy matter; do not choose me for judge.
I have said already, though I am sole king, I cannot
Act in your case without my people. May my citizens
Never, if some mischance befell us, say to me,
'You destroyed Argos for the sake of foreigners.'

CHORUS: Great Zeus, their ancestor and ours,
Sets up his finely-balanced scale,
Looks on both sides, and truly deals
Evil to the evil, blessings to the good.
Since all's now poised impartially,
Why fear to perform justice in my cause?

KING: To save us all, our need is for deep pondering;
An eye to search, as divers search the ocean bed,
Clear-seeing, not distracted, that this dilemma may
Achieve an end happy and harmless; first, for Argos
And for myself, that war and plunder may not strike
Us in reprisal; and that we may not surrender
You who are suppliants at the altars of our gods,
And so bring Vengeance, that destroying spirit, to plague
Our lives, who never, even in death, lets go his prey.
Is it not clear we must think deeply, or we perish?

CHORUS: Think! And befriend us
Justly, religiously;
Do not betray the fugitives
Whom godless men drove from their homes!
Do not see me dragged
Away from this shrine of many gods,
O King, all-powerful in Argos!

Know these men's intent
For the proud wickedness it is,
And beware the anger of Zeus.

Never endure to see your suppliant
Led like a horse by the frontlet
In defiance of justice,
From the sacred images,
And hands grasping the rich softness of my gown.
Know that your decision,
Whether for us or against us,
Remains for your children and your house;
Whatever your action towards us, good or ill,
Such will be their destiny.
Think well: this is the justice of Zeus,
And it must prevail.

KING: I have thought well; and here's the rock that strands me
    now:
With one side or the other it must come to war.
That fact, like a hull clinched with winches,* is nailed fast;
Nowhere do I see safe, untroubled harbourage.
When costly goods are jettisoned in a storm, more goods
May come by grace of Zeus, who gives increase of wealth,
And fill instead another, larger ship with freight.
So when the tongue's arrows have been untimely aimed
Word may heal word, and soothe the offended soul with
    charms.
But, to prevent shedding by kin of kindred blood,
Sacrifice must be made with prayer, and many victims
Must fall to many gods, to keep the curse at bay.
In truth I have entered this dispute to my own ruin;
But in foretelling ruin – I choose ignorance
Rather than knowledge; may good fortune prove me wrong!

CHORUS: I have said much to move your pity; but one last
    word.

KING: Speak if you wish; I am attending carefully.

CHORUS: We have sashes and girdles that we tie round our
    gowns.
KING: What of it? Are they not all women's proper wear?
CHORUS: I tell you, they will provide an admirable means —
KING: Come, now, speak clearly; what is it you are trying to
    say?
CHORUS: Unless you pledge your faithful word to all of us —
KING: Well, what of your girdles? Admirable means for what?
CHORUS: To deck these images with dreadful ornaments.*
KING: You speak in riddles. Tell me plainly what you mean.
CHORUS: Upon these holy shrines at once to hang ourselves.
KING: To hang ...! That word falls like a whip-lash on my
    heart.*
CHORUS: Your eyes are open now; I have made you see the
    truth.
KING: Yes, I see overwhelming troubles everywhere;
    Disasters press upon me like a river in flood.
    Here I am launched upon a deep and dangerous sea
    Where ruin lurks, and no safe harbour is in sight.
    Should I fail to secure for you the help you ask,
    You threaten us with pollution beyond reckoning;
    Or, if I brave your cousins, Aegyptus' sons, and take
    My stand before our walls and fight the matter out,
    Is it not in the end a bitter price to pay,
    That men for women's sake should soak the earth in blood?
    Yet Zeus protects the suppliant, and I must fear
    His anger, which of all things most is to be feared.

    Go, aged Danaus, quickly; carry in your arms
    Suppliant branches such as these your daughters hold;
    Place them on other altars of the Argive gods,
    So that the evidence of this appeal be seen
    By all our citizens; but, of me, let no word fall —
    All citizens love to find fault with government.
    It may be some will see these tokens and be stirred

To pity and indignation at these arrogant men,
And Argos grant more readily your plea for help.
Weakness wakes generosity in every heart.

DANAUS: What we prize more than many other things is this,
To have found a friend who feels for us and fears the gods.
But send some of your Argives with me to escort
And guide me, that I may find the altars of your gods
By temples in the town, or on your fortress walls,
And that I may pass safely through your streets – my dress
And person both betray me as a foreigner;
Nile breeds a race different from that of Inachus.*
Caution is best; rashness too soon may lead to fear;
Men before now have killed their friends in ignorance.

KING: That's sound advice. Go with him, men; conduct him to
The city shrines and sanctuaries of the gods.
– And don't stand talking at street-corners about this sailor
You're guiding round the temples as a suppliant.

> DANAUS, escorted by some of the KING'S bodyguard,
>   goes off in the direction of Argos.

CHORUS: Our father has your bidding; let him go. But what
Shall *we* do? What encouragement have you for us?

KING: Leave your boughs here, to show your need before the
gods.*

CHORUS: See, we obey you.*

KING: Move now to this level grove.

CHORUS: How can a grove open to all give sanctuary?

KING: I will not cast you out as prey to carrion birds.

CHORUS: What then? As prey to men more cruel than deadly
serpents?

KING: You have had kind words from me: yours should be
courteous.

CHORUS: Are you surprised if terror breeds discourtesy?

KING: Terror should be outweighed by reverence for a king.

CHORUS: Then, O king, cheer and help us with both word and
deed.

KING: Be sure your father will not abandon you for long.
   Meanwhile I go to assemble all my countrymen,
   That I may make Argos your friend; I'll also tell
   Your father what is best to say. Wait here; and beg
   Our country's gods to grant you all your heart desires.
   I go, then, to dispose matters as I have said;
   And may persuasion and success attend my words!
          Exit PELASGUS *and his bodyguard.*
CHORUS: Zeus, King of kings, among the blest most blest,
     Of sovereign powers most sovereign,
     In bliss eternal dwelling,
   Hear us, and grant persuasion and success.
   Rout the male arrogance you justly loathe;
     Plunge the pursuing Fury
     With all its swarthy oarsmen
   Deep in the storm-trough of the purple sea.

   But look with favour on our ancient race
     And on our sex, recalling
     The old and tender story
   Of her you loved, the mother of us all.
   Be full of memory, you who laid your hand
     On Io! Zeus, we claim you
     For author and begetter,
   As we claim Argos for our ancient home.

   Egypt I have left, and come
   To these meadows where long ago our mother stood,
   Where she grazed among flowers under a watchful eye.
   It was from here that Io,
   Lashed by the gadfly into madness, fled
   And passed through many tribes of men
   Till, cutting a path through the sea-waves
   Between Europe and Asia,
   She saw on either hand the neighbour continents.

Thence she fled through the land of Asia,
From end to end of the Phrygian sheep-pastures;
She reached the city of Teuthras among the Mysians,
And ascended the glens of Lydia;
Then over the Cilician and Pamphylian hills
On still she ran, to the land of Aphrodite,
A land full of wheat, and famous
For perpetual rivers and deep, rich soil.

Still frantically circling
Before the sting of the winged drover,
She came to fertile Egypt, the garden of Zeus,
To meadowlands nourished by melting snows,
And ravaged by the whirlwind,
To the waters of Nile which no disease may touch;
Still crazed with exhaustion and shame,
Wild with the destroying pain of Hera's goad.

Men of those days, inhabitants of Egypt,
Trembled at heart and were pale with terror
At a sight so unheard-of and unnatural.
They saw a creature at once human and brute,
Part cow, part woman, and were speechless at the prodigy.
And then – then, who was it comforted her,
Pitied the misery of her long wandering,
The pang of the whirling sting that tortured Io?

It was Zeus, who rules in sole and endless power.
Zeus, with tender strength,
Breathing on her the breath of godhead, brought her rest;
And, resting, she let fall in tears
The fullness of her grief and her dishonour.
Receiving in her body the 'freight of Zeus'*
(How truly said!), she gave birth
To a child without fault.

And her child had long life and all prosperity.
Therefore the whole life-giving land of Egypt
Cries, 'Certainly this is the child of Zeus.
For who but Zeus could have healed
The madness Hera's guile inflicted?
This healing is the hand of Zeus;
This child is the seed of Zeus:
Say thus, and your aim will reach the very truth.'

Which of the gods could I with reason summon
To perform an act* that with clearer right is his?
King of gods, you are our father;
Your own hand planted our stock.
Let your heart turn to memory, great maker,
Zeus all-blessed, giver of happiness.

You on your throne obey no higher command;
Yours is not the humbler authority
Deputed by an overlord; you do not bow
To the will of any enthroned above you.
Whatever purpose your pregnant mind holds
Your power can hasten to birth and to fulfilment:
You speak, and it is done.

Re-enter DANAUS.

DANAUS: Good news, my children! Argos in full assembly has
Reached absolute decisions favourable to us.

CHORUS: Welcome, my father, dearest of all messengers!
Tell us this one thing – what does their decision say?
What action is laid down by the prevailing vote?

DANAUS: The Argives have decided – and without dispute,
With one clear voice that made my old heart young again;
Why, the air was thick with the right hands of the whole city –
And this was their decision: we are to live in Argos
As free, inviolate guests, promised security
From mortal malice. Neither Argive nor foreigner

Can touch us. Should our enemies use force, the man
Who, being a citizen, does not come to our help
Will suffer loss of civic rights and banishment.
So eloquently King Pelasgus spoke for us,
Warning his people thus: 'Do not in future time
Feed full the vengeance of the god of suppliants.
Here is a twofold claim, of guests and citizens;
If we reject them, there will rise to threaten us
Twofold pollution, like a fiend insatiable
Gorging on ruin.' At this, impatient of delay,
The Argives raised their hands and voted as I have said.
The king used every subtle and persuasive turn
Of the orator's art: Zeus brought the issue to success.

CHORUS: Come, now, let us recite
A prayer for the men of Argos,
That good may reward the good they have done to us.
May Zeus, the stranger's friend,
Look upon and fulfil the grateful vows
Offered by strangers for their hosts,
That our words may attain the desired end.

Now hear my voice, you gods of heavenly birth,
While I pour out these offerings of prayer:
Never let flames leap and devour
In this Pelasgian city,
Nor lustful Ares raise his joyless clamour,
Who mows the field of man where others sowed.
For the Argives took pity on us,
And cast their votes in kindness;
They respect the suppliants of Zeus,
This sad and pitiful flock.
Not with the men they voted,
Spurning the cause of women;
They heeded the anger of Zeus
Which avenges and fulfils,

Which none can fight against,
Which no house would endure to have
Like an evil bird defiling the roof,
A visitant loaded with disaster.
Argos respects the bond of blood
And the suppliant at the pure shrine of Zeus;
Therefore their altars shall be clean,
And their offerings acceptable to the gods.

So from my lips, hallowed by these garlands,
Let eager prayer take wing,
That never may plague strip Argos of its men,
Nor civil war stain her soil
With Argive blood shed by her own citizens.
Let her flower of youth grow unplucked;
Let not Ares, Aphrodite's lover,
Man's destroyer, cut off their prime.

Let the council-seats of their old men
Be graced with venerable beards;
Thus let their city be well governed,
While they pay due reverence to Zeus,
And above all to Zeus the God of Strangers,
Who establishes Right by immemorial law.

We pray that the crops of the earth
May without fail bring forth their kind,
And that Artemis of the arrows*
May bless their women in childbirth.

May murder and devastation
Never come to tear this city,
To put a sword in the hand of Ares, father of tears,
To banish dancing and music
With the shout of civil war.

May sicknesses, that melancholy swarm,
Settle far from the homes of Argos;
And Apollo look kindly on all their youth.

May Zeus make their soil fertile
To yield its dues of fruit
And each crop in its season;
May the herds that graze across their fields
Produce young in abundance;
And the people prosper in all things
By the blessing of the gods.
May singers chant songs of piety at their altars,
While from pure lips rises the voice wedded to the string.

May their council, holding lifelong office,
Watch with wise forethought and deliberation
The people, whose power rules the State.
To foreigners in their city may they grant
Lawful appeal and honouring of contracts,
Before the sword is drawn or harm inflicted.

And may they always honour
The gods who keep their country
With the ritual they learnt from their fathers on their own
     soil,
With bearing of laurel boughs and sacrifice of oxen.
For the law of reverence to parents –
This duty is written third
In the laws of Justice, whom all must honour.

DANAUS: Dear children, I commend your wise and pious
     prayers.
Now listen; and do not tremble when you hear from me
News sudden and unwelcome. From this suppliant seat,
My look-out post, I see the ship! The rig of the sail,
The gunnel-screens* – beyond question an Egyptian craft;

The prow, with eyes that scan its forward path, obeys
The guiding rudder at the stern – too well, for us
Its victims. Ah! Now I see men on board, their limbs
Showing dark against their white clothes. Now the other ships
Are full in sight, and the whole fleet. The leading vessel,
Close under land, has furled sail, and sweeps in with oars.

Come, then, you must act calmly and advisedly;
Face what confronts you; fix your minds upon these gods.
I'll go and fetch help – men to defend and justify
Our cause. Maybe, some herald, or agents of those men,
Trying to lay hands on you as their property –
But no! That shall not happen; have no fear of them.
Still, it is best – in case our rescue were delayed –
To remember always the protection offered here.
Courage! Time and the day of reckoning will bring
Justice to every sinner who defies the gods.

CHORUS: Father, I am frightened! With what speed their ships
     have flown
   To catch us! There's but a moment between us and them.
        I am terrified and trembling;
        Is it any real advantage
        To have fled so far from home?
        Father, I am faint with dread.

DANAUS: My child, the Argives ratified their firm decree.
   Courage, then; they will fight for you, I am sure of it.

CHORUS: Aegyptus' sons are mad with lust and recklessness,
   Greedy for battle; you know well I speak the truth.
        Their ships are stoutly timbered,
        Their prows of shining metal;
        They have aimed at us and found us –
        And dark-skinned thousands at their back.

DANAUS: And thousands they shall meet to match them, strong
     in arm,
   Lean, and with muscles hardened in the mid-day heat.

CHORUS: Do not leave me alone! Father, I kneel to you.
   A woman has no courage; what can she do alone?
      And those men know no reason,
      They are madmen and blasphemers,
      And care no more for altars
      Than birds that feed on offal.

DANAUS: That is to your advantage, children, if those men
   Should merit the gods' enmity, as they do yours.

CHORUS: You think fear of the gods, of tridents, thunderbolts,
   Will hold their hands from us? I tell you it will not.
      They are arrogant and lustful,
      Swift with the force of frenzy,
      Fearless as hounds, and ready
      To mock the gods to silence.

DANAUS: The proverb says wolves have three times the
   strength of hounds;
   No byblus-fruit can be a match for ears of wheat.

CHORUS: They have the very temper of wild lawless beasts;
   We must defend ourselves – there is no time to lose.

DANAUS: A fleet takes time putting to sea, and time again
   Coming to land. No captain, even with anchor dropped,
   Dares be too hasty making hawsers fast on shore –
   A ship needs shepherding, most of all towards evening, on
   A harbourless coast. Sundown and the fall of night
   Make a good steersman sweat as if in labour pangs.
   No force can make a proper landing till their craft
   Lies happily anchored. Be discreet, then, and with minds
   Fixed on the gods, obtain their help. I'll plead for you –
   Old voice, young words: Argos shall applaud your messenger!

Exit DANAUS.

CHORUS: Mountainous land, whose royalty protects us,
   What will become of us? Where shall we fly to?
   What dark cavern will hide us?
   O to mount up like black smoke
   Close to the bright clouds of Zeus,

Or to fly wingless, invisible,
Vanish, and be lost like dust!
But flight is useless, we can escape no longer,
And my heart is darkened and trembling.
I am the prey my father's watching caught;*
I am dead with fear.
I would rather meet my fate in a drawn noose
Than give my flesh to a husband I abhor;
Sooner let Death possess me!

Could I but find a seat in the blue air
Where drifting rain-clouds turn to snow,
Some smooth summit where even goats cannot climb,
A place beyond sight, aloof,
A dizzy crag, vulture-haunted,
To witness my plunge into the abyss,
To escape a forced marriage my heart refuses!
Then my dead flesh might feed wild dogs,
Fatten the vultures of the valley, I'd be content!
For death is freed from suffering and tears.
Let death aim well,
And claim me before the bed and the embrace.
Where can I fly to be free,
To escape the bond of the flesh?

Shriek with a call heaven-high,
Offerings that the gods will hear and answer,
Prayers for deliverance!
Zeus, Father, look upon this struggle;
Justice is in your eyes:
Smile not upon violence.
Lord of the earth, All-powerful,
Have mercy on us your suppliants.
Aegyptus' sons are hunting us,
Rushing upon us with battle-cries,

With all the brutal arrogance of pursuing males,
To take us by force!
Zeus! You alone hold the beam of the balance;
Without you nothing attains its end.

Look, look! Here comes the sea-pirate!
What do you want on shore? Why have you come?

[*the Egyptian* HERALD *approaches with
a number of armed men*]

Help, help! We need help! We are calling for help!
This is the beginning:
This is the prelude to suffering and slavery.

[*as the Egyptians advance, they rush to the images*]

Help, help! Fly to the gods for help!
They are lecherous and savage;
King Pelasgus, punish them and destroy them!

Seeing the images, the Egyptians at first hesitate.

HERALD: On board, on board! Come on, now, to the ship,
Fast as your feet will take you. . . . If you won't,
We'll pull your hair out, stick daggers into you,
Till you're running with blood, blood, blood;
Then we'll cut off your heads.
Come on, plague take you; off with you to the ship!

CHORUS: I wish the huge flood of the salt sea
Had drowned you as you came,
And your outrageous masters and your brass-bound ship;
And we could have stayed happy and unmolested.
Leave violence, I tell you; quit this insane attempt;
Away, out of this sanctuary! Back to your ship,
And respect the city of Argos.

Never again may I see the Nile,
That fertilizing stream, that feeds
The blood leaping in lusty veins of Egypt!
We are of Argive race, of an ancient line,
Royal ourselves, descended from a queen.

HERALD: Talk on! But you're coming on board,
    Whether you want to or not.

CHORUS: Argives! Come to our help, come quickly!

HERALD: Come yourself, come on; or you'll be sorry
    When I lay hands on you and drag you away.

CHORUS: May *you* be dragged, you and your rogue's hands,
    Over the choppy sea; driven with Syrian gales
    On to the sandbanks by Sarpedon's tomb.

HERALD: Aye, shriek and howl and clamour for the gods;
    You can't play ducks and drakes with an Egyptian ship.
    Howl on, shriek louder; can't you sound more pitiful?

CHORUS [*amidst weeping*]: May the sea swallow you
    As you round the wooded point of Cyprus!
    May the mighty Nile, that sent you forth to wickedness,
    Record your wickedness as lost for nothing!

HERALD: Our ship's prow points to sea:
    I tell you, get on board, waste no more time.
    Dragging by the hair isn't a gentle game.

CHORUS: Father, O father, this human fiend,
    Like a spider watching its prey,
    Weaves its web to close me in.
    It is a dream; O Mother Earth, Mother Earth,
    Help me, take away this terrible dream!
    O Mother Earth, O Father Zeus!

HERALD: I'm not afraid of these gods of yours;
    I owe them nothing – birth nor life.

CHORUS: Help! This human vermin's coming for me;
    Snake that he is, he's grasped me by the foot.
    Oh, beast! Help, help, Mother Earth, Mother Earth,
    Help me, take away this terrible beast!
    O Mother Earth, O Father Zeus!

HERALD: Do as you're told, then, get on board; or else
    I'll turn nasty and tear the fine clothes off you.

CHORUS: Rulers and chiefs of Argos!
    Help, they are carrying us off!

HERALD: You'll soon have rulers enough:
  Aegyptus' sons will rule you!
  You won't be calling out for rulers, never fear!
CHORUS: We're beaten!
  [*the Egyptians take hold of the Danaids and begin to drag them
    off. Suddenly* PELASGUS *appears with an armed guard. The
    Danaids call to him while he is still at a distance*]
  King! They are dragging us from the altars!
HERALD: It seems after all I'll have to pull you by the hair,
  Since you pay no attention to a word I say.

Enter KING PELASGUS.

KING: You there, what are you doing? What sort of arrogance
  Is it, that defies Pelasgians on their own soil?
  Do you think you've come to a land of women? We are
    Greeks,
  And foreigners must learn to use greater respect.
  You'll find mistakes like this will bring you little good.
HERALD: Mistakes? What have I done that was not justified?
KING: First, you have not learnt how an alien should behave.
HERALD: Have I not? How? Because I found here what was
    lost?
KING: Did you seek Argive spokesmen to present your case?
HERALD: Great Hermes is my spokesman – god of lucky finds.
KING: You claim the gods' help – and outrage their sanctuary?
HERALD: The gods I worship live beside the River Nile.
KING: And ours, you mean, are nothing?
HERALD: I would like to see
  If anyone is going to rob me of these women.
KING: Touch them, and you'll be sorry for it on the instant.
HERALD: Your words offer no welcome to a stranger.
KING: None
  To those who violate the altars of the gods.
HERALD: I'll carry this report back to Aegyptus' sons.
KING: Your doing so will cause me no anxiety.
HERALD: But – that I may present a more informed account,

Clear in each detail, as a herald should – tell me:
My masters sent me for these women, their own cousins;
Who shall I say forced me to return with empty hands?
Not that this matter calls for courts or witnesses;
The judge is Ares, who decides such causes, not
With damages in money, but with heavy toll
Of fallen men, and limbs convulsed in bloody death.

KING: Why should I tell my name? You'll hear it in due time
And know it, you and your whole crew. As for these women,
If their goodwill were given, if pious argument
Won their consent, then you should take them; but this city
Voting in full assembly, with one mind resolved
Never to yield them up to force; and this decree
Is firmly nailed for ever, fixed immovably.
What I have said is not inscribed on wax, or sealed
In scrolls of parchment: you have heard a free tongue speak
The plain truth. Now, out of my sight immediately.

HERALD: It seems we are to undertake a dangerous war.
Then may the male cause gain the victory and rule.

KING: You'll find the men of this land too are males, and bred
On stronger drink than barley mead.

     [*the* HERALD *and his men depart*]

                  Women, take heart;
And go now with your own companions, all of you,
Into our strong-walled city, locked secure with towers
And shrewd defences.

     [*during this speech the maids attending the*
          Danaids gather on the stage]

               We have houses set aside
For public hospitality; I myself am housed
On no mean scale. In Argos you may choose to live
With others in large houses, or, if you prefer,
Alone in single dwellings; pick out, free of cost,
What suits and pleases best. And for your patron here
Take me, and all my citizens, whose resolve is thus

Given full effect. Who has more right to champion you?

CHORUS: King of Pelasgia, may every good,
Showering upon you, reward your goodness!
And, of your favour, bring here to us
Our father Danaus, that soul of confidence,
To take thought for us and guide our counsels.
He, and not we, must first consider
Where we should stay, what place will receive us kindly.
People are quick to be censorious
Of those who speak with a foreign accent.
May all prove well, and our reputation
Among the people of Argos
Be free from reproach and slander.

Exit KING PELASGUS *with his guard.*

Take your places, attendants, each with the mistress
To whom Danaus gave you
As part of her dowry, to wait upon her.

The CHORUS *again move from the stage down into the orchestra, where they are joined by their maids.* DANAUS *enters; he too is now attended by armed men.*

DANAUS: Children, offer your prayers, with sacrifice and libation,
To the citizens of Argos, as to Olympian gods!
It is they who have won decisive victory for our cause.
Our friends who rule this city listened to my appeal
With indignation against our cousins. To me they assigned
This bodyguard of spears, to assure me rank and honour,
And save my life from any secret murderous stroke*
That might pollute this land with a perpetual curse.
After such kindness, it is right that gratitude
Take place of honour in our hearts.*

And write down this
In memory – to my many lessons add one more:
The character of an unknown company is shown
By time. Against an alien, every man has slander

On the tongue's tip; one easy word may fix a smear.
I urge you then, having such bloom of comely youth
As makes men turn their eyes – do not bring shame on me.
A full ripe orchard is no easy thing to guard.
What wonder? It wakes *men's* cunning, turns them covetous,
And tempts, no less, winged and four-footed plunderers.
Just so, when Aphrodite* finds the orchard gate
Pushed wide, and sweet, ripe bodies there, she makes it
    known,
Till every man that passes, sick with longing, aims
Heart-melting glances at such virgin loveliness.
Remember, then; and let us not fall prey to that
Which we have toiled so far by land and sea to avoid;
We must not shame ourselves and please my enemies.
Two homes are offered you, one by Pelasgus, one
By the city, free of cost; in this you are fortunate.
Only hold fast to all the advice I have given you,
And value chastity more than you value life.

CHORUS: For the rest, may the Olympian gods grant us good
    luck.
As for my virgin beauty, father, have no fear.
Unless the gods have now resolved on some new plan,
My mind is firm: I will not change my former course.

    Come, then, on to the gates of Argos,
    Singing praise to the blissful sovereign gods,
    Both those who hold the city, and those who live
    By the ancient stream of Erasinus;
    And you, maidens, accompany our song.

    Let our song be of Argos and the Pelasgians;
    Let us hymn no more the flowing mouths of the Nile,
    But the rivers that pour their gentle waters
    To bestow the gift of children on this thirsty land,
    And make her soil mild with enriching moisture.

Let chaste Artemis look with pity upon us,
And marriage come not by compulsion of Aphrodite;
May such reward fall to my enemies!

MAIDS: But Aphrodite in our ritual song
  Is honoured, not forgotten. She, with Hera,
  Is closest in power to the throne of Zeus.
  But this goddess, various and subtle,
  Is honoured only with most solemn rites,
  Where, joined with their dear mother,
  Come first Desire, then soft Persuasion,
  To whose enchantments nothing can be denied;
  While Music, and the Loves who play in whispers,
  Have their parts assigned them by Aphrodite.

CHORUS: Still I fear those men's relentless rage,
  Their bitter cruelty, the bloody wars they threaten.
  Why are they so successful in pursuit,
  With a fair wind to speed their voyage?

MAIDS: What will be, will be. The purpose of Zeus
  Is a strong frontier which none can overstep.
  This marriage might well achieve its end
  In happiness greater than women have yet known.

CHORUS: From marriage with the sons of Aegyptus
  May mighty Zeus protect me.

MAIDS: That might, indeed, be best;
  But you, it seems, would alter the unalterable.

CHORUS: Why unalterable? *You* do not know the future.

MAIDS: True, who am I to behold
  The mind of Zeus, a sight unfathomable?
  Yet, in your prayers use restraint.

CHORUS: What limit do you say I should observe?

MAIDS: Towards the gods – never be uncompromising.

CHORUS: May Zeus, who rules the world,
  Save me from cruel subjection to a man I hate;
  Zeus, who set Io free from her affliction,

Whose healing hand with kindly force restored her –
May he grant victory to the women's cause!
I accept the better part of evil;
Content, if the good outweighs the bad,
If through my prayers means of deliverance be found,
And judgement side with Justice
By the will of Heaven.

SEVEN AGAINST THEBES

SEVEN AGAINST THEBES

*

CHARACTERS:

ETEOCLES, *King of Thebes*
A SOLDIER
CHORUS *of Theban women*
ANTIGONE ⎱ *sisters of Eteocles*
ISMENE ⎰
A HERALD
Six armed Champions of Thebes, and other soldiers,
citizens, and attendants

*

An open square in the city of Thebes. Some primitive images of gods
stand on pedestals. In the background the view stretches over the city
wall to the Theban plain where the besieging army is encamped.
The time is a little before dawn.

A number of citizens enter talking excitedly, and fall to a hush as
ETEOCLES *arrives, attended by a few soldiers.* ETEOCLES *wears*
the robes of a king, but is not armed.

ETEOCLES: Citizens, sons of Cadmus!* The man who holds the
    helm
Of State, and from the bridge pilots with sleepless eyes
His country's fortunes, must speak what the hour demands.
If things go well, the thanks are due to Heaven; but if –
Which Heaven forbid! – ill-luck should meet us, Eteocles
Would be the one name harped upon in every street
With threats and wailings of indignant citizens;
From all which, may Zeus the Protector now protect
The city Cadmus founded! But you too must play
Your part. The youth still short of manhood, the old man

Whose prime is past – let both, nursing their vital force
To greatness, keep watch every way as duty calls;
Guard well your city, guard the altars of her gods,
That their due honour may not perish; guard your children,
And this dear earth, your mother and your nurse; for she,
When you were crawling infants, with her kindly soil
That bids all comers welcome, nourished you, and took
The burden of your upbringing, and made of you
Trustworthy men to found homes, carry shields, and grow
In strength and worth, able to answer this day's claim.

So far, the scale of fortune weighs upon our side,
Thanks to the gods, who through this lengthy time of siege
Have given to us the best of the war. But now our prophet,*
Who keeps the augural birds and without help of fire
By hearing and reflection tells infallibly
The drift of portents – he, interpreting such signs,
Says that among the Achaeans a supreme attack
Is now this night being planned to overthrow our city.
Then, to the walls! Swarm to the battlements and gates;
Forward, full-armed; man parapets, fill every floor
Of every tower; and in the gate's mouth hold your ground
With courage. Never fear this horde of foreigners!
God will give victory. [*The citizens shout and cheer.*]
                                        I have sent scouts to survey
The enemy's army; they'll not waste their time, I trust;
With their report I shall be safe against surprise.

                        Enter a SOLDIER.

SOLDIER: Most noble Eteocles, King of the Cadmeans,
I bring reliable news from the army of the enemy,
Where I saw with my own eyes all that was going on.
Seven heroes, fierce leaders of armies, took a bull
And cut its throat, and caught the blood in a black shield,
And dipped their fingers in bull's gore, and swore an oath
In the dread name of Cruelty, of bloodthirsty Terror,

Either to annihilate the city of the Cadmeans,
Making her land a desolation, or to die
And with our soil mingle their blood. And they were bringing
To hand on Adrastus' chariot tokens of themselves
To be taken home to their parents; they shed tears, but none
Uttered a word of grief. Their hearts of iron blazed
With courage, like the blood-light in a lion's eyes.
I have not delayed bringing this news, bad as it is;
I left them drawing lots, letting the fall of luck
Decide how each should lead his troops against our gates.

Then pick at once the city's strongest fighting-men
And post them at the open gates. The entire force
Of Argos now advances on us at full speed;
The white foam from their horses' breath flecks the whole
   plain.
So be a wise ship's captain, and make all secure
Before the storm of war bursts on our city walls.
Waves of armed warriors roar on land; to meet them, use
Whatever way seems readiest. I shall keep my eyes
On watch no less by day, and bring you true reports
Straight from the field; being forewarned you'll take no harm.

Exit SOLDIER.

ETEOCLES: O Zeus, and Earth! You gods who guard this town!
   O Curse
Of Oedipus my father,* mighty in revenge!
Behold this city, whence in our Greek tongue these prayers
Flow forth: do not deliver her to her enemies
Uprooted, shattered, homes and altars laid in dust!
Never enslave this land of freedom, Cadmus' town,
With cruel chains. Come to our help. Our common cause
Speaks for us: for a prospering land honours its gods.

Exit ETEOCLES* *followed by the citizens. A moment after, the*
   CHORUS, *women of all ages, enters in a disorderly panic.*
   They look out towards the open plain.

CHORUS: Oh! I am crying with an agony of terror!
Their army is let loose; they have left camp.
Look! Here they come, streaming forward,
The horsemen at their head;
I know it by the dust rising in the air,
Which has no voice, but tells a true story plainly.

[*a distant roar is heard*]

The clatter of hoofs over the ground stuns my senses.
The sound grows nearer; it flies;
It roars with a mountain torrent's irresistible thunder!
Hear us, hear us, hear us, gods and goddesses!
Death rushes upon us;
Come to the help of our walls, protect us!
The army of white shields, with weapons trim,
Charges against our city.
What god or goddess will save or support us?
Why do I not at once fall in entreaty
Clasping the holy images?
Hear us, you who sit on the thrones of the blessed!
It is time to cling to the images; why do we wait, be-
    wildered?
Do you hear the clang of shields, or do you not?
When, if not now, should we turn to prayers,
Pleading our gifts of robes and garlands?
I dread that clanging; that rattle is of ten thousand spears.
Ares, what will you do?
Will you forsake this land, your own from the beginning?
God of the golden helmet, look down, look upon our city,
Which once you called your well-beloved.

[*the women move to the images and sit clasping them*]

Come, all you gods who guard our country;
See us, threatened with slavery, joining in supplication.
A surge of soldiers with slanting crests
Seethes around our city,
And the breath of Ares drives them on.

Then Zeus, Zeus, father, sovereign lord,
Drive back our enemies, rob them of their prey!

The Argives encircle the fortress of Cadmus;
We are terrorized with tools of war.
The bits, gripped between horses' teeth,
Are piping a song for killing;
While, spear in hand, seven leaders,
Their armour outshining all others,
Draw lots and take their stand
Each at the gate that falls to him.

And you, born of Zeus,
Strong Pallas, glorying in battle,
Be our city's Deliverer!
And you, creator of horses, king of the seas,
Poseidon, strike with your fisherman's trident,
Bring us release from terror.
And you, Ares, Ares,
Guard the city Cadmus named,
With your bright presence protect us.
You too, Cyprian goddess, mother of our race,
Help us; though we are born from your own blood,
Yet with prayers that are offered to gods
We come near and call upon you.
You too, Apollo, Wolf-god, turn wolf
To the flock of the enemy's men,
Exacting groan for groan;
And you, virgin daughter of Leto, bring forth your bow.
    [*a pause, during which all listen apprehensively; they
                break the silence by a terrified scream*]
I heard the thud of chariots!
They are circling the city. O Queen Hera!
That sound was the rattle of axles
Heavily loaded. Pity us, Artemis!
The air raves with the vibration of spears.

What is happening to our city?
What will be the event?
What is the end that God ordains?
   [*a crash is heard outside; they scream again*]
Hark! Stones showering on our parapet!
O beloved Apollo!
And in the gates the drumming of bronze-bound shields.
And you, Queen Athene,* blest in battles,
To whom Zeus gave holy authority
To decide the issue of war, stand over us,
And save your home, the city of seven gates.

Hear us, you gods perfect in power;
Hear us, sovereign gods and goddesses,
Protectors of our country's bulwarks:
Do not betray our city
Thus in the labour of battle
To enemies of alien mind.
Listen to us maidens, be just and listen
As we stretch out our hands to you in prayer.

Hear us, our own gods, and deliver us;
Stand astride our city, show her your love.
Remember the offerings of this people,
And remembering, deliver us!
Let your thoughts dwell on our city's holy rites
And her devoted sacrifices.
                    Enter ETEOCLES.
ETEOCLES: You intolerable creatures! I ask you, is this the way
   To save us? Will this encourage our fighters on the walls —
   To fling yourselves on the statues of our guardian gods
   And howl and shriek, to every sane person's disgust?
   Women! In wartime, or amid the blessings of peace,
   Save me from living among them! Give women their own way,
   They're bold past bearing; but, once they're alarmed, they
      double

Every difficulty, in the city and in the home.
Look now: by rushing panic-stricken here and there
You flood our citizens' hearts with fear and cowardice.
The enemy thus gets all the advantage he could wish,
While we inside the walls are cutting our own throats.
This is what comes of living amidst a crowd of women.

Now, anyone who disregards my authority,
Whether it be man or woman or anything between,
The stone of death* shall sentence him. Yes, he shall die
Without appeal; the people's hands shall stone him dead.
War is for men, and words from women are not wanted.
You have no place out here; get indoors, where you can do
No harm. Do you hear, or do you not? Or are you deaf?

CHORUS: Dear son of Oedipus, what frightened me was the
    sound
  Of the thud and rattle of chariots,
  The shriek of the axles and the rolling wheels,
  The harsh tune of the helms
  That hold horses by the mouth,
  The fire-forged bits that curb them.*

ETEOCLES: Then does the steersman labouring in a heavy sea
  Abandon his wheel and rush for safety to the prow?

CHORUS: No – but I trust the gods; therefore it was to them,
  To these ancient statues, that I ran headlong
  When I heard on our gates the drumming of that deadly hail.
  Yes, terror drove me then
  To pray to the blessed ones
  To hold a protecting arm over our town.

ETEOCLES: Pray that our walls hold firm against the enemy's
    spear.*
  Is that not to the gods' advantage? For they say
  That when a town is taken all her gods depart.

CHORUS: May I not live to see
  This full council of gods desert us,

94

    Foreign soldiers swarming in our streets,

    Tearing, burning, destroying.

ETEOCLES: Pray, if you will; but why abandon common sense?

    Where does the proverb say Safety is to be found?

    Her mother is Obedience, wife of the Deliverer.

CHORUS: It is true; but the strength of gods is higher still;

    And often, when men are helpless in disaster,

    When dark clouds hang over their eyes,

    Even out of the most stubborn griefs

    The help of Heaven shows them the way.

ETEOCLES: The service of the gods, blood-offerings, sacrifice

    For divination, these are men's concern, when they

    Try strength with the enemy; yours is to stay quiet at home.

CHORUS: By the gods' help we live in an unconquered city,

    And our wall keeps out hordes of our enemies.

    The gods are not angry because we pray to them.

ETEOCLES: I have no objection to your honouring the gods;

    Only be calm and quiet, and don't give way to terror;

    You'll spread despondency among our citizens.

CHORUS: The sudden confused sounds of war frightened me;

    And I ran in panic here to the Acropolis,

    The sacred home of gods.

ETEOCLES: Listen: if you hear of men dying and wounded, do not

    Seize on the news with shrieks. Men's blood is Ares' diet.

CHORUS: There! I hear horses neigh!

ETEOCLES: Don't be too keen of hearing.

CHORUS: Our fortress groans from the ground! They are encircling us.

ETEOCLES: No doubt. I'll deal with that – leave everything to me.

CHORUS: I am afraid. The crashing at the gates grows louder.

ETEOCLES: Silence! We want no talk like that about the town.

CHORUS: You gods who share our life! Do not forsake these walls.

ETEOCLES: Plague take you! Will you not be patient and hold
your tongues?

CHORUS: O gods, we are your people; save us from slavery.

ETEOCLES: It is you who are making slaves of me and of us all.

CHORUS: Almighty Zeus, take aim against our enemies.

ETEOCLES: Zeus, what a gift you gave us when you created
women!

CHORUS: Women suffer as men do if their city's captured.

ETEOCLES: With hands on holy images you speak such words?*

CHORUS: I have lost my courage; terror carries away my
tongue.

ETEOCLES: I appeal to you: don't force me to use harsher
measures.

CHORUS: We don't know what you want; explain to us.

ETEOCLES: I want you
To hold your miserable tongues, and not dismay your friends.

CHORUS: We will. Fate is the same for all; we will endure it.

ETEOCLES: This tone pleases me better. Now do even more:
Stop clinging to these statues; make a better prayer,
That the gods will fight for us. First listen to my vows,
Then raise with good heart the strong cry of victory,
The shout of sacrifice familiar to all Greeks,
To inspire our men and make them fearless in the field.

I for my part vow to our country's guardian gods
Who keep watch on our fields and on our city's streets,
To the fountain of Dirce and to the river Ismenus,
That if the day be ours, and this city delivered,
The altars of our gods shall run with blood of sheep,
Bulls shall be slaughtered to them, trophies dedicated,
Robes of our enemies. Listen to my words, you gods:
'Robes of our enemies, spoil of battle gashed with swords,
I will hang up as garlands in your holy temples.'
That is how you should pray; not with these loud laments,
Nor blurting foolish barbarous words before the gods;
Which certainly won't save you from what is to be.

Meanwhile I'll choose six men, and then return, and post
Them, with myself as seventh, to guard our seven gates,
Matching the enemy in pride and strength; otherwise
The roar of hasty rumour will reach all our people
And fill them with a fever of ill-advised alarm.

Exit ETEOCLES.

CHORUS: I heed you; but my mind is alert with fear.
Anxiety, neighbour to my heart,
Kindles dread of the hordes that encircle us;
As a trembling dove dreads
For the sake of the young in her nest
The snake which cruelly creeps into their bed.
See, where they advance towards our ramparts,
Fighters of every sort, a nation in arms!
What will become of us?
See again, they hurl jagged stones in a shower
Against our men harried by sword and sling.
You gods of heavenly birth,
Put forth every power
To save the city and race that Cadmus planted.

What habitable country will you find better than this
If you give up to the enemy this deep soil of ours,
And the spring of Dirce, most nourishing of all waters
Which Poseidon, Encircler of the earth,
And the children of Tethys pour out for men to drink?

Therefore, you guardian gods,
Hurl down havoc on the army at our gates,
Slaughter of men, throwing away of shields;
And win for yourselves glory among our people.
Be saviours of our city,
Make firm your thrones among us,
In answer to our loud laments and prayers.

How pitiful that a town of unremembered age
Should thus be condemned to perish,

97

Captured by the sword, enslaved,
A heap of crumbling cinders,
Left desolate and dishonoured
By the hand of the Achaean and the will of the gods;
That widowed women young and old
Should be led like horses by the hair,
And their clothes in rags about them;
As the ruins are evacuated a cry rises,
The mingled voices of prisoners going to their fate.
It is a dreadful future that I fear.

And tears must flow for girls gently bred
Who before the marriage rite has gathered their maiden flower
Travel the hateful road to new homes.
What of them? I say that the dead
Enjoy a happier lot.

When a city is defeated
There are many pains and miseries to be met;
One man captures or kills another;
They bring fire and the whole place is foul with smoke.
The madness of Ares masters men in masses,
And breathes defilement over all reverent feeling.

A din of shouting fills the streets;
The fence of bastions fails;
Man faces man and falls before the spear.
Stained with blood, mothers of new-born infants
Cry for their young slaughtered at the breast;
Roving bands tear apart those of the same family.
Plunderer meets plunderer, both loaded;
Empty-handed calls empty-handed
To try fortune with him, discontented
Either with less or with equal shares.
'You can see for yourself,' they say,
'If you're left behind, who waits for you?'

Stores of all kinds of food litter the ground at random —
A sight to sadden a good housewife;
Bountiful gifts of the earth thrown heedlessly together
Float down the flood of reckless waste.
And the young women, now slaves, and new to sorrow,
Prizes of war, a pitiful bed awaits them,
The bed of a man whose fortune is to have conquered his
     enemy;
There with the night they will come to their initiation,
Their comfort for pain and never-ending tears.

CHORUS 1: Dear friends, look! Surely that's the soldier coming
     back
With something new to tell us from the battlefield;
He runs as fast as if his feet were chariot-wheels.*

CHORUS 2: Here is the king himself, the son of Oedipus,
Arriving just in time to hear the messenger's news;
He too quickens his stride with sense of urgency.

Enter from one side the SOLDIER; *from the other* ETEOCLES
     attended by the six Champions and other soldiers.

SOLDIER: I know exactly the dispositions of the enemy;
I can tell you who is posted to each gate by lot.
At the Proetid Gate Tydeus already stands and roars;
But cannot yet cross the Ismenus, being forbidden
By the prophet, for the victims were not favourable;
And Tydeus, mad with lust for battle, like a snake
Shrieking at noon, belabours with abusive shouts
The prophet, son of Oecles* — skilled, he says, at scraping
Out of death's way, too coward-hearted even to fight.
With shouts like these he tosses three tall shadowing plumes,
His helmet's mane, while from the inside of his shield
Bells wrought in bronze send forth a terrifying clang;
And on the front this insolent device: a sky
Blazing with stars is there engraved, and in the centre
Shines forth pre-eminent among the stars, seeming
The very eye of night, the glorious full moon.

Thus madly exultant in his boastful panoply
He shouts beside the river-bank, lusting for fight,
Like a fierce chariot-horse* that snorts against the bit,
Chafing in expectation of the trumpet's blast.
Whom will you set against him? Who is trustworthy
To keep the Gate of Proetus when the barrier falls?

ETEOCLES: What a man wears about him will not frighten me;
Pictures can deal no wounds, his crests and bells won't bite
Without his spear. As for this *night* you tell us of,
This gleam of heavenly stars that grows upon his shield –
Such folly may well prove prophetic for a man.
What if the night of death fell on his eyes? I think
This boastful emblem would with justice vindicate
Its meaning for the very man who bears it, and
His pride become a prophecy against himself.

To fight with Tydeus, here is Astacus' brave son;
Him I appoint as champion of this gate. His birth
Is noble; he reveres the throne of Modesty,
And hates proud speech; laggard in any shameful act,
But not in deeds of war. A young branch sprung from those
Whom Ares spared of the Sown Men* is Melanippus,
Son of our soil indeed. The event Ares will settle
By the luck of the throw; but this is certain: it is Justice,
Goddess of kindred's duty, whose law sends him forth
To protect the earth that bore him from an enemy's sword.

Exit MELANIPPUS.

CHORUS: Then may our champion, who goes forth
In Justice's name to fight for our city,
Be granted victory by the gods.
But I tremble with fear to see
The bloody deaths of men
Who die fighting for their loved ones.

SOLDIER: So may the gods grant Melanippus victory!
The Electran Gate has gone by lot to Capaneus,*

A giant-like boaster worse than him already named.
His bragging shows pride more than human; and he hurls
Against our walls strange, fearful threats, which Heaven
    frustrate.
God willing, God unwilling, he will sack this town,
Says he; and not the counterblast of Zeus himself,
Cast at his feet, will stop him; lightnings, thunderbolts,
He thinks no more of than of the sun's mid-day heat.
And for device he has an unarmed fire-bearer
Whose weapon is a blazing torch gripped in both hands,
Whose words, in golden letters, are 'I'll burn this town'.
Send, then, to challenge such a hero – who will go?
Who will stand up to him, unmoved by all his boasts?

ETEOCLES: With him too our advantage grows from gain to
    gain.
When men's pride swells in folly, then their tongue becomes
Their true accuser. Capaneus' threats are not mere words –
He is prepared to *act* defiance to the gods.
In crazy exultation, with his lungs' full strength,
He sends his mortal challenge up to heaven, his words
Swelling like waves to thunder in the ear of Zeus.
And I am sure his fire-bearer will come to him
As he deserves – the thunderbolt, not comparable
To the sun's mid-day heat. Against him I have set a man
Grudging of speech, fiery in courage, Polyphontes;
Whose strength will be our sure protection, by the grace
Of Artemis* our Champion and of other gods.

[*exit* POLYPHONTES]

Now name another, with the gate assigned to him.

CHORUS: Death to the loud boaster against our city!
May the thunderbolt be the weapon that halts him,
Before he bursts into my home
And with his insolent spear
Makes its maiden retreats a desolation!

SOLDIER: Now for the next to draw the gate he should attack.

The third lot leaping from the upturned bronze helmet sent
Eteoclus to hurl his troops against the Neïstan Gate.
His restless mares, eager to charge the entrance, toss
Their frontlets as he turns them now this way, now that.
Their muzzle-pipes, filled with the proud beasts' breath, sound out
A savage music. On his shield is a device –
No humble one: a man in armour climbing up
By a ladder to the enemy's wall to sack their town;
And this man too shouts – and his words are written there –
'Ares himself shall not repulse me from their walls!'
Against him too send out a man whom we may trust
To keep our country from the chains of slavery.

ETEOCLES: Here is the man at once: I will send Megareus,
Of the Sown race, and son of Creon – one whose hands
Will do his boasting for him. Let him be our choice,
And luck go with him. No wild din of snorting horses
Will drive *him* trembling from the gate. Either in death
He'll pay his debt for nurture to his native soil,
Or, conquering two men and a fortress on a shield,
He'll carry home his spoils to grace his father's house.
Come, give us the next champion's brag, leave nothing out.

CHORUS: Defender of our homes!
We pray for success to our cause,
And death to our enemies.
As in their mad pride
They boastfully threaten our city,
So may Avenging Zeus look upon them in anger.

SOLDIER. The fourth, who has drawn the gate next to Athena Onca*
Comes with a shout to take his stand: Hippomedon,
A tall and splendid figure; believe me, when I saw
His great round threshing-floor of a shield, and watched him spin it,
I shook. That was no shoddy workman who bestowed

Such craftsmanship upon his shield. The emblem shows
Typhon, his mouth with fiery breath belching black smoke
Which glitters, almost flame;* and there are coils of serpents
Running around the rim, to clamp the outer case
Fast to the framework of the hollow-bellied circle.
He has raised his battle-cry; Ares has entered into him;
A Bacchant, drunk with lust of war – his eye strikes terror.
Take good care who is to try the measure of such a man;
Already at our gates the boast is Panic Rout.*

ETEOCLES: First, Onca Pallas, neighbour to our city gate,
Who hates man's arrogance, will baffle this cold snake
Seeking her nest and brood. Second, Hyperbius,
Brave son of Oenops, is a man to match this man.
Willing, when picked, to learn his part from the hour's need,
He bears a body, spirit, and arms, all qualified
For this encounter. Hermes did well to match these two;
The man is enemy to the man whom he will meet,
And on their shields the gods whom they will match together
Are likewise enemies – one has Typhon breathing fire,
While on Hyperbius' shield sits, unmoved, Father Zeus,
The fire-bolt flaming in his hand. No man, I think,
Has seen Zeus worsted. Such are the gods who favour them;
And we are with the winning, they the losing side,
Since in a battle Typhon has less strength than Zeus.
If we may hope, with men thus matched, that victory
Will answer to their emblems, then Hyperbius
Will know the saving hand of Zeus, whose shield he bears.

CHORUS: My faith is that the antagonist of Zeus,
Who bears on his shield the figure of Typhon
The earth-born, the unloved,
A picture hateful alike to unseen powers,
To the human race, and to immortal gods –
That there before our gates his head will hit the dust.

SOLDIER: May that prove true! Next I will speak of the fifth man,
Stationed at the Borraean Gate, close by the tomb

Of Amphion, son of Zeus. He swears by the spear he holds –
Which in his confidence he values above God
Or his own eyes – that he'll destroy the city of Cadmus
Even in spite of Zeus. This is the way he talks –
This rosy-cheeked cub of a wild hill-roaming woman,
A man half-boy; why, only now, over his cheeks
Is spreading the lush springtime crop of curly hair.
Yet his advance shows pride not maidenish like his name*
But savage, and his eye is grim. There at our gate
He stands, and not without his brag; his bronze-bound shield,
Rounded in shape, protecting his whole body, flaunts
An insult to our city: the gleaming embossed figure
Of a cannibal Sphinx, pivoted ingeniously,
And made to move. And under her she carries a man,
One of our Cadmeans – a taunt to draw upon this fighter
The full weight of our weapons. He has not come, I reckon,
To trade piecemeal in fighting, but to justify
His lengthy journey – he's from Arcadia: Parthenopaeus.
That is your man; an alien, who in Argos found
Shelter and noble breeding; now, to pay his debt
He hurls against these walls threats which may Heaven
    frustrate.
ETEOCLES: May they, their blasphemies, their boastful em-
    blems, all
Meet at Heaven's hand the violence of their own rage!
Ruinous and evil, like themselves, would be their end.
But for him too, the Arcadian whom you describe, we have
A man: no boaster, but his hand looks to the deed –
Actor, the brother of the last chosen champion.
He will not let this flood of deedless talk flow in
To water weeds; nor let an enemy whose shield
Depicts that loathsome monster pass within our gates.
The Sphinx shall blame her bearer, when she finds herself
Under our ramparts rammed and hammered outside in.*
And may my every word be truth, with Heaven's goodwill.

CHORUS: I am struck to the heart's core,
      My hair stiffens in horror,
      When I hear of the proud speech
      Of these proud-mouthed and impious men.
      May the gods, if they be gods,
      Destroy such men in battle.

SOLDIER: Sixth I must name a soldier who refrains from boasts,
      A prophet who fights bravely, strong Amphiaraus.
      Stationed at the Homoloean Gate he pours abuse
      Upon great Tydeus: 'Murderer, public trouble-maker,'
      He cries, 'who more than all taught Argos evil ways,
      High priest of bloodshed, wakener of avenging spirits,
      Adrastus' counsellor in this infatuate war.'
      Next, with his gaze upturned to heaven, he calls aloud
      On him whom birth has made your brother, Polyneices,
      'Seeker of Strife' – twice dwelling on that ominous name;*
      And speaks thus: 'Surely such a deed pleases the gods,
      Is glorious both to hear and hand on to the young –
      To bring an alien army to assault and ravage
      Your fathers' city, lay in dust your country's gods!
      Can it be right to quench the spring that nursed your life?
      When your own soil is made the prisoner of your sword
      Because you are jealous, how can that assist your cause?
      For me, it is this country's earth I shall enrich;
      My tomb and oracle shall stand on foreign ground.
      Then let us fight. I foresee death, but not dishonour.'
      So spoke the prophet, holding motionless his shield
      Of solid bronze. And on its circle was no sign;
      For he cares not to seem the bravest, but to be;
      Harvesting thus the fertile furrow of his mind,
      From which grow such sound counsels. As a match for him
      I advise you send a warrior both wise and brave;
      A man who reverences the gods is to be feared.

ETEOCLES: Well may one curse the chance that couples man
      with man,

Pious with impious, good with bad. There is nothing worse
In any enterprise than evil company;
Its harvest is no blessing; for when folly ploughs,
The crop is death. A good man, maybe, joins a ship
Where wickedness is purposed by a guilty crew,
And shares the fate of men whose kind the gods abhor;
Or in the city, a good man, cast among the bad
Who oppress strangers and forget the gods – he too,
Though innocent, is caught in the same trap as they,
And tamed and disciplined by Heaven's impartial scourge.
Just so this prophet Amphiaraus, a modest, brave,
Upright, and pious man, a powerful seer, allied
Against his judgement with blaspheming, boastful men
In a far journey that shall prove long to retrace –
He, if Zeus will, with them shall be dragged down to earth.

Indeed, I think he will not even attack the gates;
Not through despair or cowardice; but he knows well
What end awaits his fighting, if Apollo's word
Is to bear fruit; and the god's way is to keep silence
Or else speak truth. Yet we will match him with a man,
Strong Lasthenes, an inhospitable gate-keeper;
He has an old man's wisdom, a young man's muscle; an eye
Alert as his nimble foot; a spear-arm quick to pounce
On the uncovered spot beside his enemy's shield.
Yet – among mortals victory is the gift of Heaven.
CHORUS: Hear our prayers, O gods;
Grant what we justly ask:
Give victory to our city.
Turn the peril of the sword
Upon those who invade our land.
While they are still outside our battlements
May Zeus with his thunderbolt
Strike them and kill them!
SOLDIER: I'll tell now of the seventh man at the seventh gate–

Polyneices, your own brother. Upon Thebes and you
He calls down curses and destruction; prays that he,
Standing upon our walls, proclaimed as conqueror,
Chanting over our land wild shouts of victory,
May fight with you, and, killing you, die at your side;
Or, should you live (cries he) who have so dishonoured him
With exile, may he take a like revenge on you
And banish you as he was banished. Thus he shouts,
Calling on gods of kindred and of fatherland
To bear him witness and respect these prayers of his —
Brimful of strife and violence, true to his name!

The shield he has is newly built, a perfect round;
On it a twofold emblem, cleverly contrived:
A full-armed warrior is displayed in hammered gold;
A woman leading him goes modestly before.
'Justice' she says her name is, as the lettering
Will show; 'And I'll bring back this man from banishment.
He shall possess a city, and in his father's home
Go to and fro at pleasure.'   Such are the devices
They carry with them. It is for you now to decide
Whom you will send. I'll take the message – that's my duty;
But you're our city's captain: you must choose the man.
ETEOCLES: O house that gods drive mad, that gods so deeply
        hate,
O house of endless tears, our house of Oedipus!
It is his curse that now bears fruit in us his sons.
Yet there's no time for either tears or groans, for fear
This agony bear interest more crushing still.
For Polyneices – truly named – we shall soon know
What truth is in his blazon, whether he can win
Return from banishment by letters of wrought gold
Flaming across his shield, joined with insanity.
If Zeus's virgin daughter, Justice, ever had
Smiled on his acts and thoughts, he might have won return.

But neither when he escaped the darkness of the womb,
Nor as a child, nor when he first reached manhood, nor
When the hair of his beard grew thick, ever by word or look
Would Justice acknowledge him. Now, surely, least of all,
When his own city suffers violence at his hand,
Does Justice stand beside him. Should she join with one
So infatuate, Justice would herself be named a lie.

    In this faith I will go and face him – I myself.
Who has a stronger right than I? Chief against chief
I'll match him, brother to brother, enemy to enemy.
[*to an attendant*] Run, bring my greaves,* to protect me
    against spear and stone.
SOLDIER: Never, beloved master, son of Oedipus!
    Why must your mood match with your brother's blas-
    phemies?
    It is enough that Cadmeans fight hand to hand
    With men of Argos; blood so shed can be appeased.
    But your two bloods are one: such brother-murdering –
    Not through an age of time could that pollution fade.
ETEOCLES: If fate must be endured, let it come free from
    shame;
    What else is there to glory in, among the dead?
    But doom joined with dishonour strikes our last hope dumb.
CHORUS: My son, what are you bent upon?
    Do not let bursting passion
    And lust for battle carry you away.
    This urge that you feel is evil –
    Banish it before it grows.
ETEOCLES: This act moves swiftly to a head; Heaven wills it so;
    Then let the wind of doom, Hell's tide, and Phoebus' hate*
    Bear down to ruin Laius' race to the last man.
CHORUS: You are goaded on by a wild craving
    For a ritual of blood; but the fruit will be bitter,
    For the flesh that you tear is man's flesh,

And the blood is not lawful.

ETEOCLES: Yes, to this ritual my own father's wicked curse
Appoints me, haunting me with dry pitiless eyes,
Assuring me that death is better soon than late.

CHORUS: Refuse to listen! Your prosperity once established,
You will not be called a coward. Will not
The black-cloaked spectre of the house depart
When the gods accept offerings from your hand?

ETEOCLES: The gods, I am sure, have already ceased to think
of us.
The offering they desire from us is that we die.
Why any longer shrink from our appointed end?

CHORUS: Give way now, while there is time.
Even yet the wind of the gods' enmity,
After so long, may turn,
And favour you with a milder breath;
Though now it rages as before.

ETEOCLES: This rage was kindled by the curse of Oedipus.
How true a prophet is that figure of my dreams
Who comes each night to apportion our inheritance!

CHORUS: Let a woman's words persuade you even against your
will.

ETEOCLES: Say what you have to say, and finish; no long speech.

CHORUS: Go anywhere, I beg you, but to the seventh gate.

ETEOCLES: My will is set; not all your words can blunt it now.

CHORUS: Even unvaliant victory wins the gods' approval.*

ETEOCLES: That is no motto for a man in arms to accept.

CHORUS: Are you prepared to plunder your own brother's
blood?

ETEOCLES: When the gods send destruction there is no escape.
Exit ETEOCLES.

CHORUS: I tremble at the Power who brings a whole race to
ruin,
The god unlike other gods,
Infallible in foretelling evil,

The Erinys invoked by a father's curse;
See her now fulfilling the angry prayers
That Oedipus in his frenzy uttered;
She is this hatred which we see
Driving Oedipus' sons to destroy each other.

And the stranger apportioning their inheritance,
That Chalybus who comes from distant Scythia
To be a harsh divider of their possessions,
Is cruel-hearted steel;
It is steel that has cast the die and assigned them land –
As much as dead men may hold;
But in these spreading plains they have no share.

When men die by a kinsman's hand,
When brother is murdered by brother,
And the dust of the earth drinks in
The crimson blood that blackens and dries,
Who then can provide cleansing?
Who can wash it away?
O house, whose guilty agonies,
The old vintage and the new, mingle together!

For I speak of a sin sown long ago –
Which brought swift punishment then,
Yet now abides to the third generation –
When Laius disobeyed Apollo,
Who from his Pythian shrine at the world's navel
Three times in oracles warned him,
If he would save his city,
To die without issue.

Mastered by the rashness of love
He begot for himself, to his own doom,
The father-killer Oedipus,
Who sowing seed in the forbidden field,
His mother's womb in which he grew,

Endured the bloody harvest of his act;
For the spirit of madness brought them together,
And their understanding was taken from them.

And troubles followed like a sea rolling its waves onward;
One breaks, and it lifts the next, three heaped together,
Whose surge seethes around our city's hull;
And our barrier between life and death
Is no more than the width of a wall;
I fear for Thebes and her line of kings,
Lest all be overwhelmed together.

When a curse arising from an ancient oracle
Falls due, the settlement is heavy;
The forces of ruin are active, and will not pass by.
And when men who live by bread prosper and grow too great,
Then to lighten the ship
They pay their toll from the depth of the hold.

What man was ever as highly honoured
By gods or by fellow-townsmen in the crowded square
As they honoured Oedipus
On the day when he freed our country
From the Fiend that preyed on human flesh?

But when, wretched man, he became aware
Of the miserable marriage he had made,
Tormented and outraged, in the madness of his heart,
With the hand that killed his father he doubled his own
    suffering:
He destroyed those eyes
That could not bear to see his children.

And when his sons grudged him his place at home,
Then in fury and with a bitter tongue, alas!
He hurled curses upon them,
That in time they should apportion their inheritance

With violence and a dividing sword.
And I tremble lest at this moment
The hotfoot Erinys may fulfil his curse.

Enter a MESSENGER.

MESSENGER: Courage, you children trembling at your mothers'
knees!
Our Thebes is safe from slavery! Those proud men's boasts
Have fallen to nothing. Thebes has reached calm after storm.
No leak let in those battering waves; our wall is sound;
For men of trust fought back our enemies and stood
Like barricades before our gates. And all is well –
For the most part – at six gates; but the seventh gate
The Lord Apollo, he the dread Commander of Seven,*
Took for himself, and so brought Laius' ancient sin
To due fulfilment for the race of Oedipus.

CHORUS: What happened? Is there some new terror for our
town?

MESSENGER: The town is safe. But the two sons of Oedipus –

CHORUS: What of them? I am bewildered – I am afraid to hear –

MESSENGER: Come, now, keep calm and listen. Oedipus' two
sons –

CHORUS: O misery! I cannot help guessing the worst.

MESSENGER: Both equally, and utterly –

CHORUS: To the bitter end?
It is grief, yet tell me.

MESSENGER: Both are dead. They killed each other.

CHORUS: Each too much like his brother in the lust to kill.

MESSENGER: Each like the other in the fate that led them both,
That fate which now annihilates their ill-starred race.

The event, then, gives us matter both for joy and tears:
Our city thrives; but her two heads and generals
Have thus divided with forged Scythian steel the sum
Of their inheritance. The land that they possess
Shall be what each gets for his grave – whither they go

Borne down on the ill wind of their sad father's curse.
So, Thebes is saved. But her two brother kings are fallen;
The earth has drunk their blood, shed by each other's hands.

Exit MESSENGER.

CHORUS: O mighty Zeus, and gods who guard our city,
True deliverers of these walls of Cadmus!
Am I to be glad and shout for joy
That Thebes has escaped unhurt?
Or shall I weep for our leaders in war —
Pitiful, ill-fated, childless —
Who, true to their name* and full of enmity,
Were destroyed by their own sinful purpose?

CHORUS 1: O curse of the race, O curse of Oedipus,
Dark and unrelenting!
A dreadful coldness falls about my heart:
The song that I sang in my frenzied vision,
When I heard of men bleeding and miserably dying,
Was a song for burial — surely an ill omen
To sing such a song in a time of battle!

CHORUS 2: Not so; but the curse their father uttered
Exacted its due without reprieve;
Laius' disobedience was the cause of all.
No anxious care for the city
Can keep at bay what prophets have foretold.
O you whom all must weep for,
Have you done this unbelievable thing?
Is this no rumour, but the pitiful truth?

[*a procession is seen approaching with the bodies
of* ETEOCLES *and* POLYNEICES]

See! This sight speaks plainly; no herald is needed.
Here we may see the mutual murderous ends
Of two joined in one doom that breaks our hearts.
What else is here but grief, the child of grief,
At last returning to its rightful home?

Come, friends; bring your sighs for a fair wind,

The beat of hand on head for the plash of oars –
The familiar rite which sends over Acheron
That sacred ship* with black sails and no wreaths of flowers
To the land Apollo may not tread,
That welcomes all alike,
Where no sun lightens the gloom.

> [*the bodies are set down.* ANTIGONE *and*
> ISMENE *approach*]

Look! Antigone and Ismene* are here;
They have a bitter duty, to mourn for their brothers.
I know that with all sincerity
The sorrows of their sweet breasts
Will be uttered in full and worthy lamentation.
But before they speak it is our duty
To cry aloud the hymn of the Fiend of Doom
And to chant the hated triumph-song of Death.

Ah, you who are more unhappy in your brothers
Than all who bind their gowns across the breast!*
I weep and groan; not from pretence
But truly from the heart my shrill cry comes.

CHORUS 1: Alas, perverse men,
Whom your dear ones could not persuade,
Whom wickedness could not weary!
With all your pitiful courage,
What you have overthrown is your father's house.

CHORUS 2: Pitiful indeed; who, to destroy their house,
Won for themselves a pitiful death.

CHORUS 1: Alas [*to* POLYNEICES] you who cast down walls –
The walls of your own home!
Who [*to* ETEOCLES] achieved a monarch's throne –
To your own harm!
[*to both*] Now you have settled your quarrel with the sword.

CHORUS 2: The dread Erinys of your father Oedipus
Has with exactness fulfilled his curse.

CHORUS 1: See where they were struck – both on the left
  side.

CHORUS 2: Struck indeed – bodies that grew from one flesh!

CHORUS 1: Alas, they were possessed!

CHORUS 2: Alas, they were cursed,
  Doomed to mutual murder!

CHORUS 1: The blow of Fate they suffered
  Was mortal to both house and life,
  Enforced by their inexpressible rage –

CHORUS 2: And by the impartial doom
  Their father's curse brought down upon them.

CHORUS 1: Throughout our land the sound of mourning
  spreads;
  The city's bastions mourn;
  The soil mourns for the men it loved.
  All Thebes unclaimed waits for new heirs –
  Thebes, for whose sake they died –

CHORUS 2: For whose sake their strife went on to its mortal
  end.

CHORUS 1: With eager hearts they shared their inheritance,
  Jealous for their just portion;
  And their arbiter* is not held blameless
  By those who loved them –

CHORUS 2: And no thanks are given to Ares.

CHORUS 1: Blades of iron brought them where they lie;
  Blades of iron shall soon
  Part for them their father's land.
  – What land? How parted? one may ask.
  – Both shall share his grave.

CHORUS 2: As we say farewell to them
  Our loud lament rends our hearts;
  Our cries are spontaneous, our sorrow is our own.
  In the anguish of our thoughts there is no joy,
  Our tears flow from hearts that waste away
  As we weep for these two princes.

CHORUS 1: Unhappy pair! We may record of them
　　That they provided for their citizens
　　And for aliens of every rank
　　A costly, ruinous banquet of death.

CHORUS 2: It was a hard destiny their mother had –
　　More than all women who are called mothers of children.
　　She took her own child to become her own husband;
　　These are the sons she bore; this is their end.
　　Hands which grew from the same seed
　　Have destroyed each other's life.

CHORUS 1: These who grew from the same seed
　　Now together are sown upon the ground,
　　And their race with them.
　　They divided their living with the edge of enmity,
　　And in mad jealousy their quarrel reached its end.

CHORUS 2: Now their enmity is over; and their lives mingle
　　Where a pool of gore soaks into the earth;
　　Now they are truly of one blood.
　　He was a harsh settler of quarrels,
　　The stranger from the sea who leaps out of fire –
　　Iron ground to an edge;
　　And a harsh and cruel divider of possessions
　　Is Ares, who makes a father's curse come true.

CHORUS 1: Poor souls, they have their portion –
　　The measure of a man – which God bestows;
　　But under their bodies will be
　　An unfathomed amplitude of earth.

CHORUS 2: Ah, you who have wreathed your race
　　With garlands of many griefs!
　　At the end of the day victory belongs to the Curses,
　　Who shout in shrill triumph
　　Over the utter rout of the defeated house.
　　At the gate where they fought stands Ruin's trophy;
　　And their Fate overthrew them both
　　Before he would hold his hand.

ANTIGONE *and* ISMENE *now move to centre stage to mourn over the bodies.*

ANTIGONE: If you gave wounds, you also received wounds.

ISMENE: If you dealt death, you also suffered death.

ANTIGONE: With the spear you killed –

ISMENE: By the spear you died –

ANTIGONE: Pitiful in inflicting.

ISMENE: Pitiful in suffering.

ANTIGONE: Let the cry rise –

ISMENE: Let the tear fall –

ANTIGONE: For you who died.

ISMENE: For you who killed.

ANTIGONE: My heart is wild with sobs.

ISMENE: My soul groans in my body.

ANTIGONE: Brother, whom I weep for –

ISMENE: Brother, most pitiable –

ANTIGONE: You were killed by your brother.

ISMENE: You killed your brother.

ANTIGONE: Twofold sorrow to tell of –

ISMENE: Twofold sorrow to see –

ANTIGONE: Sorrow at the side of sorrow!

ISMENE: Sorrow brother to sorrow!

CHORUS: O Fate, whose gifts are cruel and grievous,
    O august shade of Oedipus,
    O dark Erinys, how great is your power!

ANTIGONE: This is a sad and terrible sight.

ISMENE: This is how I welcome him from exile.

ANTIGONE: And when he killed, he failed to gain his home.

ISMENE: And when he saved his home, he lost his life.

ANTIGONE: He lost his life.

ISMENE: And took his brother's.

ANTIGONE: O reckless sons!

ISMENE: O hopeless end!

ANTIGONE: The same sad name for both.

ISMENE: The same tears for a threefold agony.

117

CHORUS: O Fate, whose gifts are cruel and grievous,
    O august shade of Oedipus,
    O dark Erinys, how great is your power!
ANTIGONE: You know now that you sinned –
ISMENE: You learnt in the same moment –
ANTIGONE: When you came back to Thebes.
ISMENE: When you chose to fight your brother.
ANTIGONE: How terrible a tale!
ISMENE: How terrible a sight!
ANTIGONE: Alas, for suffering!
ISMENE: Alas, for wrong done –
ANTIGONE: To the royal house and to Thebes –
ISMENE: To me even more.
ANTIGONE: Alas for the consummation of follies and miseries!
ISMENE: Alas for the most tormented of mankind –
ANTIGONE: Who in their folly –
ISMENE: Were like men possessed.
ANTIGONE: What place shall we find to bury them?
ISMENE: Where they will receive most honour.
ANTIGONE: Alas, alas!
    If they sleep by their father they will trouble him.

Enter a HERALD.

HERALD: I am to proclaim the pleasure and decree of those
    Who are regents for the people of this Cadmean city.
    It is decreed that Eteocles, in recognition
    Of his devotion to this city, shall be interred
    In his own native soil; for in her cause he chose
    To defy his enemies at cost of his own life;
    Thus, guiltless towards the temples of his father's gods,
    He died with honour where it befits young men to die.
    Regarding him, that is my message. For his brother
    Polyneices here, his body is to be thrown out
    Unburied for dogs to tear – he who would have destroyed
    This Cadmean town, had not some god stood in his way
    With his brother's spear. So he shall bear even in death

The pollution of his sin against his father's gods,
Whom he – this man – insulted, launching a foreign force
Upon our town to overthrow it. His reward
Shall be dishonour, vagrant birds his only tomb;
No troops of slaves shall heap the earth above his corpse,
No shrill melodious dirge be chanted in his honour,
Nor any funeral rite performed by next of kin.
For him, such is the fate authority decrees.

ANTIGONE: And I reply to your 'authority' in Thebes:
If no one else will join with me in burying him,
Then I will bury him, and chance what danger may
Result from burying my own brother. Nor am I
Ashamed to disobey thus and defy the State:
Another call, from the one flesh that made us both –
Sad mother's, ill-starred father's – will not be denied.
Therefore, my heart, gladly like a true sister stand
By him in wretchedness, the living by the dead.
My brother's flesh no hollow-bellied wolf shall tear –
And let no man decree it! Woman as I am,
I will contrive a grave for him, and dig the earth
And carry it in the fine cloth of this costly gown,
And bury him with my own hands; and no decree
Shall stop me. Never fear but I shall find the way.

HERALD: I warn you, do not think you can defy the State.

ANTIGONE: I warn you not to herald me – you waste your time.

HERALD: A people newly freed will show an ugly mood.

ANTIGONE: Then ugly be it. My brother shall not lack his grave.

HERALD: Will you honour with burial a public enemy?

ANTIGONE: The gods settled long since what honours are his right.

HERALD: Not if since then he plunged this land in mortal fear.

ANTIGONE: He had been wronged. He was but answering wrong with wrong.

HERALD: Because one man had wronged him, he attacked us all.

ANTIGONE: Strife is, of all the gods, longest in argument.
   Make no more speeches. I am going to bury him.
HERALD: Take your own counsel; but you have been warned by
   me.

Exit HERALD.

CHORUS: Alas, alas!
   You proud triumphant Erinyes, spirits of evil,
   Destroyers of families, who have thus cut off
   Root and branch the stock of Oedipus!
   What will happen? Which side can I take?
   What solution can I find?
   How can I bear not to weep for you,
   Not to follow you to your grave?

   But I am afraid;
   I shrink from the anger of the citizens.
   You, Eteocles, will find mourners in plenty;
   Shall he, poor soul, depart unlamented,
   With dirge from none but his own sister?
   Who would consent to that?
CHORUS 1: Let the State do, or not do, as it will.
   We here will follow Polyneices to his grave,
   And take part in his burial.
   This sorrow belongs to the whole race of Cadmus;
   And what a State upholds as just
   Changes with the changing of time.
CHORUS 2: And we will go with Eteocles;
   Since here the State and Justice speak with one voice.
   For it was he above all
   Who, after the blessed gods and almighty Zeus,
   As pilot of our Cadmean city,
   Saved us from overturning
   And from being engulfed in the wave of foreign invaders.
         The bodies are carried out to left and right,
            half of the CHORUS *following each.*

THE PERSIANS

THE PERSIANS

*

*

The royal palace of Xerxes at Susa; the tomb of Darius. Time: 480
   B.C., *or early in 479; a few months after the battle of Salamis*
   (September 480).
Enter the CHORUS, *venerable Councillors of the Persian king.*

CHORUS: We are the Persian Council, left in trust,
   For all our Persians serving now in Hellas,
   To guard this rich and golden house. The King,
   Xerxes himself, son of Darius, chose
   Our rank and years to govern his domain.

   But when will they return – Xerxes our king
And all his gold-clad armament? Our hearts
Heave in our breasts, clamouring prophetic fears.
The flower of Asian youth left home; and none,
Runner nor rider, brings us word of them.

   From Susa, from Ecbatana,
   From ancient Kissian ramparts,
      From each ancestral door,
   The Persian force flowed westward –
   Seamen in ships by thousands,

And horsemen, footmen, marching
    In the stiff ranks of war.

Captains of Persian valour,
The Great King's kingly servants,
Amistres, Artaphernes,
Megabazes, and Astaspes,
    Press to their distant goal;
Masters of bow and bridle,
A sight to daunt the senses,
A shock to numb the muscles
    With hardiness of soul;
Artembares, whose chariot
Ran rife with death; Masistres;
Imaeus, that brave bowman;
The fearless Pharandaces;
Sosthanes, whose four horses
    Flew in his firm control.

Next from the Nile there gathered
(That vast and fecund water)
Yet others: Susiscanes,
Pegastagon, Arsames
Ruler of holy Memphis;
And Ariomardus, giver
Of laws to Thebes the ancient;
And last, those skilful oarsmen,
The numberless marsh-dwellers,
    Filled the Egyptian roll.

A swarm of soft-skinned Lydians
Marched with the rest, comprising
    The mainland tribes entire,
Whose zeal their royal generals
Arcteus and Mitrogathes,
    And Sardis' gold, inspire;

While rank on rank advancing
Of three- and four-horse chariots
    Blench every face with fear.
The men of sacred Tmolus,
Bold Tharybis and Mardon,
    Those anvils of the spear,
With the light Mysian lancers,
Vow to cast down proud Hellas
    And bring her bondage near.

From Babylon the golden,
Like spate of mingled waters,
    More varied hordes appear:
Sailors who trust in timber;
Archers whose valiant fingers
    Draw arrows to the ear.
From every realm of Asia
The East in arms pours forward;
The king's dread word is spoken:
    A million sabres hear.

Such was the flower of manhood,
The pride of Persian valour,
    That we saw march away;
For whom the land that nursed them
Now grieves with ardent longing
    And counts each empty day
That quakes our hearts, and lengthens long delay.

Long since, the king led his destroying ranks
Over the strait to Europe's neighbour ground;
Crossed Helle's channel with a road that floats,
A ribbon of lashed timbers and nailed planks
Yoking the sea's neck in a bridge of boats.

Thus the Great King, in one impetuous bound,
Launches this myriad flock, this prodigy

Of armies, in two sweeps, by land and sea,
Against the whole earth; his resolve made bold
By all his captains' fierce fidelity;
Himself the peer of gods, whose race was sown in gold.*

From the darkness of his glance
Glares a gory dragon's eye.
See his thousand oars advance!
See ten thousand arrows fly!
The royal chariot rides before;
Asia's conquering bows defy
Hellene spearmen famed in war.

For when armies in their pride
Like a vast flood leap and roar,
Then no fame in war so sure
As can stem that ocean-tide;
No strong bulwark so secure.
Persian arms no strength can stay;
Persian hearts no fear can sway.

Yet, while Heaven with tortuous plan
Works its will, what mortal man
Can elude immortal guile?
Where is he whose nimble leap
Lightly clears the enclosing net?
Smooth Delusion's flattering smile
Leads but where her trap is set;
There man pays his mortal debt:
Doom has caught what death will keep.

Long ago the heavenly Powers
Laid upon the Persian name
Terms: to seek *on land* her fame;
Din of horsemen, crash of towers,
Sack of cities – these were ours.

But we learnt another skill,
Trespassed on forbidden sight,
Where the storm-wind, howling shrill,
Whips the sea's broad channels white;
Confident, a million swords
Marched to war on hempen cords.*

These are the shapes of gloom
That cloak my heart in fear
For all our men gone forth,
Lest our great city hear
That man-devouring doom
Has stripped our native earth;
Lest Susa's ancient stones
And the high Kissian wall
Echo with frenzied groans
Of women for their dead,
Beating of breast and head,
While rending fingers fall
On robes of finest thread.

Gone, like a swarm of bees,
Is our whole Persian force,
Vanished both foot and horse
Over the narrow seas –
Our bound of empire, spanned
By boats from land to land –
Whither their leader please.
While here, each Persian wife,
Longing for him she sped
Armed to the fierce campaign,
Sprinkling her empty bed
With tender tears in vain,
Weeps out her lonely life.

Come, Persians, gather by this ancient stair
Of Xerxes' palace. Counsel is our need,
Wisdom, and courage. How does Xerxes fare?
What fortune speeds the royal heir
Of Perseus, founder of our Persian breed?
Has the drawn bow made Hellas quail?
Or did the strength of bronze-head spears prevail?
            [enter ATOSSA, attended, in a chariot]
Look! The king's mother, radiant as the eyes
Of gods immortal, Queen Atossa, stands!
Fall prostrate, Persians, at her feet; then rise
And with one voice salute her. Hail, our queen,
Noblest of women in all eastern lands,
Darius' wife and Xerxes' mother, hail!
Mother of a god thou art, and wife hast been –
Unless the Fates today have turned their hands
Against us, and their ancient favour fail.

ATOSSA: That fear is mine; I too am torn by anxious thoughts.
Therefore I have left the golden-furnished chamber which
I shared with King Darius, to tell you my own dread,
That our vast wealth may in its rash course overturn
That fair peace which Darius built with Heaven's help.
Two thoughts born of this fear fill my uneasy mind,
Yet shrink from words: first, that a world of wealth is trash
If men are wanting; next, that men who have no wealth
Never find Fortune smiling as their strength deserves.
Here, wealth suffices; but our fear lies in our love:
What has a house more precious than its living lord?
How matters stand, you know; for this anxiety
Give me your counsel, Persians, old and trusted friends;
For all my hope of honest counsel rests in you.

CHORUS: Your word, great queen, is our command, whether
      to act
Or speak, as it may please your puissance to direct.
With our good counsel take our loyalty and love.

127

ATOSSA: Since first my son marshalled his army and set forth
   To waste Ionia, every night dreams visit me;
   But never yet so clear a vision as I saw
   This night that's past. Listen: two women, finely dressed,
   One in the Persian style, the other Dorian,
   Appeared to me, flawless in beauty, and in gait
   And stature far excelling women of our day.
   Sisters of one race, each had her inheritance,
   One Greece, the other Asia. And, it seemed, these two
   Provoked each other to a quarrel; and my son
   Restrained and tamed them, yoked them to his chariot,
   And fastened harness on their necks. And one of them,
   Proud of these trappings, was obedient to the rein.
   The other struggled, tore the harness from the car,
   Threw off the bridle, snapped the wooden yoke in two.
   My son fell to the ground; and by his side his father
   Darius stood and pitied him. Xerxes looked up,
   Saw him, and tore his robe. Such was my dream by night.
   I rose, and dipped my hands in the clear-flowing spring;
   Then, purified, went to the altar-hearth, to pray
   For deliverance from evil, and make sacrifice
   To those whose due it is. And as I stood, I saw
   An eagle fly for refuge to Apollo's hearth.
   I watched, speechless with terror; then a falcon came,
   And swooped with rushings wings, and with his talons clawed
   The eagle's head; it, unresisting, cowered there,
   Offering itself to wounds.
                            These signs have struck my eyes
   With dread, your ears no less. For – be assured of this –
   If my son conquers, he will be all men's wonder; but,
   If he should fail, no 'State' can hold him answerable.
   Winner or loser, while he lives he is Persia's king.
CHORUS: Lady, we would not speak to cause you undue fear,
   Nor to raise hope. Pray humbly to the gods, and ask
   Them to avert what evil omens you have seen,

And to fulfil the good, for you and for your son,
For Persia too, and all your friends. Next you must pour
To Earth and to the dead, libations; and entreat
Your lost husband Darius, whom you saw this night,
To send to you and Xerxes blessing from the depths,
And all that is not blessing to keep shrouded thick
In subterranean darkness. This our counsel springs
From loyal hearts and sober judgement; we predict
That, be these omens good or bad, all will be well.

ATOSSA: First thoughts are truest. You, my first interpreter,
Have read my dream propitiously, both for my son
And for the royal house. May all be for the best.
I will return, and will, as you prescribe, perform
These rituals for the gods and the beloved dead.
But tell me: where, by men's report, is Athens built?

CHORUS: Far westward, where the sun-god sinks his fainting
fires.

ATOSSA: But why should my son yearn to make this town his
prey?

CHORUS: Athens once conquered, he is master of all Hellas.

ATOSSA: Have they such rich supply of fighting men?

CHORUS: They have;
Soldiers who once struck Persian arms a fearful blow.

ATOSSA: Besides their men, have they good store of wealth at
home?

CHORUS: They have a spring of silver treasured in their soil.

ATOSSA: And are they skilled in archery?

CHORUS: No, not at all:
They carry stout shields, and fight hand-to-hand with spears.

ATOSSA: Who shepherds them? What master do their ranks
obey?

CHORUS: Master? They are not called servants to any man.

ATOSSA: And can they, masterless, resist invasion?

CHORUS: Yes!
Darius' vast and noble army they destroyed.

ATOSSA: To those whose sons are with the army now, your
    words
  Bring fearful thoughts.
CHORUS: If I mistake not, you will soon
  Know the whole truth. That runner's undeniably
  A Persian courier; good or bad, he'll bring us news.

Enter a MESSENGER.

MESSENGER: O cities of wide Asia! O loved Persian earth,
  Haven of ample wealth! One blow has overthrown
  Your happy pride; the flower of all your youth is fallen.
  To bring the first news of defeat's an evil fate;
  Yet I must now unfold the whole disastrous truth:
  Persians, our country's fleet and army are no more.

CHORUS: O grief, and grief again!
  Weep, every heart that hears,
  This cruel, unlooked-for pain.

MESSENGER: Yes; all that mighty armament is lost; and I
  Still see the light, beyond all hope, and have come back.

CHORUS: Why have we lived so long?
  The harvest of ripe years
  Is new grief, sudden tears.

MESSENGER: Sirs, I was there; what I have told I saw myself;
  I can recount each detail of the great defeat.

CHORUS: Lament and weep! In vain
  Went forth our army, strong
  In arrows, sabres, spears,
  To Hellas' holy soil.

MESSENGER: The shores of Salamis, and all the neighbouring
    coasts,
  Are strewn with bodies miserably done to death.

CHORUS: Weep and lament! Our dead
  Are made the ocean's spoil,
  Tossed on its restless bed,
  Their folded cloaks spread wide
  Over the drowning tide.

MESSENGER: Our bows and arrows were no help; there, over-
　　whelmed
　　By crashing prows, we watched a nation sink and die.

CHORUS: Lament with loud despair
　　The cruel and crushing fate
　　Of those whom the gods' hate
　　Condemned to perish there.

MESSENGER: What name more hateful to our ears than
　　Salamis?
　　Athens – a name of anguish in our memory!

CHORUS: Most hateful name of all –
　　Athens! Who can forget
　　Our Persian women's debt –
　　Innocent tears that fall
　　For husband lost, or son,
　　Long since at Marathon?

ATOSSA: Good councillors, I have kept silence all this while
　　Stunned with misfortune; this news is too terrible
　　For narrative or question. Yet, being mortal, we
　　Must endure grief when the gods send it. Therefore stand
　　And tell the whole disaster, though your voice be choked
　　With tears. Who is not dead? And whom have we to mourn
　　Among our generals, whose post death leaves unmanned?

MESSENGER: Xerxes the king lives.

ATOSSA: 　　　　　　　　　Then the light of hope shines forth
　　Like white dawn after blackest darkness, for my house.

MESSENGER: But Artembares, marshal of ten thousand horse,
　　Floats, bruised by the hard rocks of the Silenian shore.
　　A spear struck Dadaces, captain of a thousand men,
　　And with an airy leap he hurtled from his ship.
　　Tenagon, a true Bactrian born, first in their ranks,
　　Now haunts the sea-worn fringe of Ajax' island home.*
　　Three more, Lilaeus, Arsames, and Argestes,
　　Struck down, were seen eddying round the Isle of Doves,*
　　Butting the granite rocks. Metallus the Chrysean,

131

Who led ten thousand foot and thirty thousand horse,
Called the Black Cavalry – when he was killed, the hair
Of his thick shaggy yellow beard was dyed blood-red,
Dipped in the crimson sea. Magus the Arabian
Is dead; and Bactrian Artames has stayed abroad,
A settler in a rugged land; and Tharybis,
Captain of five times fifty ships, a Lyrnean born,
Is dead – his handsome face met an unhandsome end,
Poor wretch, unburied. Syennesis, the bravest man
In the whole army, leader of the Cilician troops,
Who with his single arm destroyed more enemies
Than any other, won great glory, and is dead.
Such is the roll of officers who met their fate;
Yet I have told but few of many thousand deaths.

ATOSSA: Alas! Here is the very crown of misery;
For Persia, shame and loss and anguish of lament.
But come, retrace your story now, and tell me this:
What was the number of the Hellene ships, that they
Dared to assault our fleet, and charge them prow to prow?

MESSENGER: Had Fortune favoured numbers, we would have
    won the day.
Three hundred vessels made the total Hellene strength,
Not counting ten picked warships. Xerxes had, I know,
A thousand in command, of which two hundred and seven
Were special fast ships. That was the proportion. Now,
Do you say we entered battle with too weak a force?
No. The result shows with what partial hands the gods
Weighed down the scale against us, and destroyed us all.
It is the gods who keep Athene's city safe.

ATOSSA: What – safe? Is Athens then not ravaged after all?

MESSENGER: While she has men, a city's bulwarks stand un-
    moved.

ATOSSA: Now tell me how the two fleets fell to the attack.
Who first advanced, struck the first blow? Was it the Greeks,
Or my bold son, exultant with his countless ships?

MESSENGER: Neither, my queen. Some Fury, some malignant
    Power,
  Appeared, and set in train the whole disastrous rout.
  A Hellene from the Athenian army came and told
  Your son Xerxes this tale: that, once the shades of night
  Set in, the Hellenes would not stay, but leap on board,
  And, by whatever secret route offered escape,
  Row for their lives. When Xerxes heard this, with no thought
  Of the man's guile, or of the jealousy of gods,
  He sent this word to all his captains: 'When the sun
  No longer flames to warm the earth, and darkness holds
  The court of heaven, range the main body of our fleet
  Threefold, to guard the outlets and the choppy straits.'
  Then he sent other ships to row right round the isle,
  Threatening that if the Hellene ships found a way through
  To save themselves from death, he would cut off the head
  Of every Persian captain. By these words he showed
  How ignorance of the gods' intent had dazed his mind.

    Our crews, then, in good order and obediently,
  Were getting supper; then each oarsman looped his oar
  To the smooth rowing-pin; and when the sun went down
  And night came on, the rowers all embarked, and all
  The heavy-armed soldiers; and from line to line they called,
  Cheering each other on, rowing and keeping course
  As they were ordered. All night long the captains kept
  Their whole force cruising to and fro across the strait.
  Now night was fading; still the Hellenes showed no sign
  Of trying to sail out unnoticed; till at last
  Over the earth shone the white horses of the day,
  Filling the air with beauty. Then from the Hellene ships
  Rose like a song of joy the piercing battle-cry,
  And from the island crags echoed an answering shout.

    The Persians knew their error; fear gripped every man.
  They were no fugitives who sang that terrifying

Paean, but Hellenes charging with courageous hearts
To battle. The loud trumpet flamed along their ranks.
At once their frothy oars moved with a single pulse,
Beating the salt waves to the bo'suns' chant; and soon
Their whole fleet hove clear into view; their right wing first,
In precise order, next their whole array came on,
And at that instant a great shout beat on our ears:
'Forward, you sons of Hellas! Set your country free!
Set free your sons, your wives, tombs of your ancestors,
And temples of your gods. All is at stake: now fight!'
Then from our side in answer rose the manifold
Clamour of Persian voices; and the hour had come.

        At once ship into ship battered its brazen beak.
A Hellene ship charged first, and chopped off the whole stern
Of a Phoenician galley. Then charge followed charge
On every side. At first by its huge impetus
Our fleet withstood them. But soon, in that narrow space,
Our ships were jammed in hundreds; none could help another.
They rammed each other with their prows of bronze; and
        some
Were stripped of every oar. Meanwhile the enemy
Came round us in a ring and charged. Our vessels heeled
Over; the sea was hidden, carpeted with wrecks
And dead men; all the shores and reefs were full of dead.

        Then every ship we had broke rank and rowed for life.
The Hellenes seized fragments of wrecks and broken oars
And hacked and stabbed at our men swimming in the sea
As fishermen kill tunnies or some netted haul.
The whole sea was one din of shrieks and dying groans,
Till night and darkness hid the scene. If I should speak
For ten days and ten nights, I could not tell you all
That day's agony. But know this: never before
In one day died so vast a company of men.

ATOSSA: Alas! How great an ocean of disaster has

Broken on Persia and on every eastern race!

MESSENGER: But there is more, and worse; my story is not
    half told.

Be sure, what follows twice outweighs what went before.

ATOSSA: What could be worse? What could our armament
    endure,

To outweigh all the sufferings already told?

MESSENGER: The flower of Persian chivalry and gentle blood,

The youth and valour of our choice nobility,

First in unmoved devotion to the king himself,

Are sunk into the mire of ignominious death.

ATOSSA: My friends, this evil news is more than I can bear. –
How do you say they died?

MESSENGER: Opposite Salamis

There is an island – small, useless for anchorage –

Where Pan the Dancer treads along the briny shore.

There Xerxes sent them, so that, when the enemy,

Flung from their ships, were struggling to the island beach,

The Persian force might without trouble cut them down,

And rescue Persian crews from drowning in the sea:

Fatal misjudgement! When in the sea-battle Heaven

Had given glory to the Hellenes, that same day

They came, armed with bronze shields and spears, leapt from
    their ships,

And made a ring round the whole island, that our men

Could not tell where to turn. First came a shower of blows

From stones slung with the hand; then from the drawn bow-
    string

Arrows leapt forth to slaughter; finally, with one

Fierce roar the Hellenes rushed at them, and cut and carved

Their limbs like butchers, till the last poor wretch lay dead.

This depth of horror Xerxes saw; close to the sea

On a high hill he sat, where he could clearly watch

His whole force both by sea and land. He wailed aloud,

And tore his clothes, weeping; and instantly dismissed
His army, hastening them to a disordered flight.
This, then, brings you new grief to mingle with the first.*

ATOSSA: Oh, what malign Power so deceived our Persian
   hopes?
My son, marching to taste the sweetness of revenge
On Athens, found it bitter. Those who died before
At Marathon were not enough; Xerxes has won
For us not vengeance but a world of suffering.
But tell me now, what of those ships that have escaped?
Where did you leave them? Have you any certain news?

MESSENGER: The captains of surviving ships spread sail and
   fled
In swift disorder with a following wind. On land
The remnants of the army suffered fearful loss,
Tortured by hunger, thirst, exhaustion. Some of us
Struggled at last to Phocis and the Melian Gulf,
Where cool Spercheius wanders through the thirsty plain.
We came next to Achaea; then to Thessaly,
Half dead for want of food; and there great numbers died
Of thirst and hunger, for we suffered both. From there
We reached Magnesia, Macedonia, and the ford
Across the river Axius, and the reedy marsh
Of Bolbe, and Mount Pangaeus in Edonia.
That night some god woke Winter long before his time;
And holy Strymon was frost-bound. Men who before
Were unbelievers, then fell on their knees in worship
Of earth and heaven; and from the whole army rose
Innumerable prayers. Then over the firm ice
They made their way. Those of us who began to cross
Before the sun had shed abroad his sacred beams
Were saved. But soon his rays shone out like piercing flames,
Melting the ice in mid-stream. Helplessly they slipped,
Men heaped on men, into the water. He who died
Quickest, was luckiest. The handful who survived,

Suffering untold hardship, struggled on through Thrace
To safety, and now at last have reached their native earth.

So, well may Persia's cities mourn their young men lost.
I have spoken truth; yet all I have told is but a part
Of all the evil God sent to strike Persia down.

CHORUS: O fatal Spirit of Destruction, cruelly
You have attacked and trampled the whole Persian race.

ATOSSA: Our army is destroyed and gone. O bitter grief!
O vivid dream that lit the darkness of my sleep,
How clearly you forewarned me of calamity!
And, Councillors, how lightly you interpreted!
Yet, since you counselled me to pray, I am resolved
First to invoke the heavenly gods; then in my house
To prepare meal and oil and honey, and return
And offer them as gifts to Earth and to the dead.
What's done, I know, is done; yet I will sacrifice
In hope that time may bring about some better fate.
You meanwhile must take counsel on our present loss
With other faithful Councillors; and if my son
Returns while I am absent, comfort him, and bring him
Safe to the house, lest his despair heap grief on grief.

Exit ATOSSA *with her attendants, and the* MESSENGER.

CHORUS: Thy hand, O Zeus our king, has swept from sight
The boastful pride of Persia's vast array,
    And veiled the streets of Susa*
    In gloomy mists of mourning.
Now countless women, partners in one grief,
With soft white hands tearing their veils in two,
    Bedew their folded bosoms
    With tears like rivers flowing;
And new-made brides turn from their silken beds
Of youth and pleasure and soft luxury,
    With tender sighs bewailing
    Their young lords taken from them,

While anguish eats like hunger at the heart.
  With them we join in mourning
  The fate of those departed.

Hear this accusing groan that rises now
From every Asian land laid bare of men:
  Who led them forth, but Xerxes?
  Who sealed their death, but Xerxes?
Whose error sent our all to sail in ships,
  And lost it all, but Xerxes'? –
Son of Darius, the invincible
  Leader of Persian bowmen,
  Belov'd by all his people!

Landsmen and seamen both had put their trust
In hulks with canvas wings and sea-blue eyes;
  And ships from home conveyed them,
  And ships at last destroyed them –
Ships, handled by Ionians, beaked with death;
  The king himself escaping
  By weary winter journeys
With his bare life across the plains of Thrace.

And those who were the first to die,
Now, helpless, left behind perforce,
Are swept along the Cychrean shore.*
Lift loud your griefs to heaven, and cry
With bitter anguish, vain remorse,
Till heart is weary, flesh is sore.

There, threshed by currents' eddying motion,
Unsightly lie those well-loved forms,
Now feasted on by voiceless swarms,
The children of the untainted ocean.
Here, every house bewails a man,
And parents, childless now, lament

The troubles that the gods have sent
To end in grief their life's long span.

From east to west the Asian race
No more will own our Persian sway,
Nor on the king's compulsion pay
Tribute, nor bow to earth their face
In homage; for the kingly power
Is lost and vanished from this hour.

Now fear no more shall bridle speech;
Uncurbed, the common tongue shall prate
Of freedom; for the yoke of State
Lies broken on the bloody beach
And fields of Salamis, which hide
The ruins of our Persian pride.

Enter ATOSSA, *alone.*

ATOSSA: Good friends, those who have learnt what suffering is,
     know this:
When waves of trouble burst on us, each new event
Fills us with terror; but when Fortune's wind blows soft
We think to enjoy the same fair weather all our lives.
Now, ringed with fears, in every threat I see Heaven's wrath;
My ears are dinned with notes that bear no healing spell;
So terribly has this ill news staggered my mind.
Therefore on foot and unattended I have come
Back from the palace, with propitiatory gifts
For my son's father, such as soothe departed souls:
Milk, sweet and white, from an unblemished cow; the gleam
Of flower-confected honey; lustral water, drawn
From virgin springs; and, from the fields, this unmixed
     draught,
The quickening essence of its ancient parent-vine;
Here, too, is fragrant oil from the pale olive, which
Thrives in perpetual leaf; and last, these garlands, twined
With flowers, the children of the all-producing earth.

So, friends, assist now this libation to the dead;
With solemn chants summon Darius from his grave,
While I, in honour of the gods who rule below,
Pour out these gifts to sink into the thirsty ground.
CHORUS: Yours be it, royal lady, Persia's dread,
　　To pour wine-offering to the mansioned earth;
　　　　While we with songs importune
　　　　Guides of dead souls for favour.

Hear, King of Shades, and all you nether Powers,
Hermes, and Earth: send up this soul to light;
　　　　For he alone, Darius,
　　　　May know, beyond our wisdom,
Some cure, and teach us how to save our land.

And does our blessed, godlike king now hear
　　　　Our strong entreaty, sung
With varied notes of agony and fear
　　　　In the hard Persian tongue?
Or must we make our crying griefs resound
　　　　To pierce the heedless ground
　　　　And wake Darius' ear?

O listen, all you lower Powers, and Earth:
　　　　Grant that that godlike head
　　　　Whom Susa brought to birth,
　　　　That august spirit, may rise;
O send him, from the depth where now he lies,
Whose like lay never yet among the Persian dead.

　　　　Dearly we loved Darius;*
　　　　Dearly his tomb is cherished,
　　　　Where now his heart lies hidden,
　　　　　　Whose thoughts to us were dear.
　　　　Release him, Aïdoneus!
　　　　Send up our godlike monarch!
　　　　　　Dread Aïdoneus, hear!

Never did King Darius
By war's devouring folly
Send countless souls to hell.
   'Wisdom of God' we called him;
And, by God's wisdom guided,
He led his people well.

King of old days, our Sultan!* Come, appear!
Stand on your tomb's high crest, king of our king,
Robed in the royalty you used to wear,
The saffron shoe, the royal diadem!
Darius, Father and Preserver, hear
Our tale of endless, nameless suffering!
Darkness and dread descend with Stygian wing:
Our young men – death has seized and swallowed them.
Darius – Father, Lord, Preserver – hear!

O King whose loss is mourned with love and tears*

Our three-banked ships are ships no more, no more!
                The GHOST OF DARIUS *rises.*
DARIUS: Elders of Persia, you who once were young with me,
   Most faithful Councillors, what task distracts our State?
   Why is the groaning earth rutted and scarred? I see
   My wife visit my tomb, and fear bids me receive
   Favourably her libations. You too at my tomb
   Stand weeping, and with shrill and anguished litanies
   Invoke my parted spirit. So, though the ascent
   From Hades is no easy journey, and the Powers
   Of Earth are readier to receive than to let go,
   Yet, since I share majesty among them, I have come.
   Speak quickly, for I may not overstay my time.
   What sudden burden of distress weighs Persia down?
CHORUS: Reverence forbids us look upon your face;
   Reverence forbids us in your presence speak;
   Now as before we dread your majesty.

DARIUS: Yet, since your supplications called me up from earth,
    Put by your dread of majesty, make no long tale,
    But in brief words deliver what you have to say.

CHORUS: For reverence we dare not do your pleasure;
    For reverence we dare not speak before you;
    For loyalty we would not speak to grieve you.

DARIUS: Then, since remembered fear restrains my coun-
    cillors,
    Speak, Queen Atossa, royal partner of my bed;
    Cease these laments and tears, be plain. Grief is man's lot,
    And men must bear it. Sorrows come from sea and land;
    And mortal ills will multiply with mortal years.

ATOSSA: Surely your happiness excels all other men's:
    Blest in your life – who, while you still beheld the sun,
    Lived long unclouded years as Persia's envied god;
    And envied now in death, which has not suffered you
    To see the abyss of ruin. Then hear all in brief:
    Persia's great name and empire are laid low in dust.

DARIUS: But how? By stroke of pestilence? or civil war?

ATOSSA: No; but near Athens our whole army was destroyed.

DARIUS: Tell me, which of my sons campaigned so far afield?

ATOSSA: Xerxes, whose rashness emptied Asia of its men.

DARIUS: Poor fool! Was it by land or sea he attempted this?

ATOSSA: Both; he advanced two-fronted to a double war.

DARIUS: How could he, with so huge a land-force, cross the
    sea?

ATOSSA: He chained the Hellespont with ships, to make a road.

DARIUS: That was a feat! He closed the mighty Bosporus?

ATOSSA: He did. Doubtless some god helped him achieve his
    plan.

DARIUS: Some god, I fear, whose power robbed Xerxes of his
    wits.

ATOSSA: Too clearly true; witness the ruin he achieved.

DARIUS: What happened to his armies, that you weep for
    them?

ATOSSA: Disaster to the fleet destroyed his force on land.

DARIUS: Destroyed? Is our whole army killed to the last man?

ATOSSA: Such is the desolation for which Susa mourns.

DARIUS: A noble army lost, the safeguard of our land!

ATOSSA: And every Bactrian, all their flower of youth, is gone.

DARIUS: O wretched son, to lose so fine an allied force!

ATOSSA: Xerxes alone, we hear, with some few followers —

DARIUS: What fate fell to him in the end? Is he alive?

ATOSSA: He reached at last, with joy after despair, the bridge
Yoking two continents —

DARIUS: Safe on to Asian soil?

ATOSSA: Safe, without doubt; the message vouches for his life.

DARIUS: How swiftly came fulfilment of old prophecies!
Zeus struck within one generation: on my son
Has fallen the issue of those oracles which I
Trusted the gods would still defer for many years.
But heaven takes part, for good or ill, with man's own zeal.
So now for my whole house a staunchless spring of griefs
Is opened; and my son, in youthful recklessness,
Not knowing the gods' ways, has been the cause of all.
He hoped to stem that holy stream, the Bosporus,
And bind the Hellespont with fetters like a slave;
He would wrest Nature, turn sea into land, manacle
A strait with iron, to make a highway for his troops.
He in his mortal folly thought to overpower
Immortal gods, even Poseidon. Was not this
Some madness that possessed him? Now my hard-won wealth,
I fear, will fall a prey to the first plunderer.

ATOSSA: Xerxes the rash learnt folly in fools' company.
They told him you, his father, with your sword had won
Gold to enrich your children; while he, like a coward,
Gaining no increase, played the warrior at home.
He planned this march to Hellas, this vast armament,
Swayed by the ceaseless slanders of such evil men.

DARIUS: Hence this disaster, unforgettable, complete;

Measureless, such as never yet made desolate
Our Persian land, since Zeus first gave this ordinance,
That one man, holding throne and sceptre, should be lord
Over all Asia's pastured plains. Medus first led
This nation; next, his son, whose wisdom ruled his will,
Performed the kingly office. Cyrus the Fortunate
Was third; who, while he governed, blessed the land with
    peace.
He added to his empire Lydia and Phrygia;
Ionia he subdued by force; and he incurred
No anger of the gods, because his heart was wise.
Fourth in succession, Cyrus' son governed the land.
Fifth, Mardus, who disgraced his realm and ancient throne;
But the brave Artaphernes with his friends conspired
And killed him in his palace. Last, I gained the place
I wished for. Many troops I had, many campaigns
I led; but never dealt my land a blow like this.
Xerxes my son is young, and has a young man's mind;
All my instruction he forgets. Be sure of this,
My Councillors: look, and you will not find that all
We Persian kings together did her so much harm.

CHORUS: Then, King Darius, what conclusion shall be drawn
    From all that you have said? How, after this reverse,
    Shall we and Persia now take action for the best?

DARIUS: By taking none. Even if your force be twice as great,
    Never set arms in motion against Hellene soil.
    You cannot win; the land itself fights on their side.

CHORUS: Fights on their side? But how?

DARIUS: Their soil is lean, and kills
    With famine any force of more than moderate size.

CHORUS: But we will send a picked force, easily supplied.

DARIUS: Not even those troops that still remain in Hellas shall
    Come safely home.

CHORUS: What? Will not all our army cross
    The Hellespont?

DARIUS: Few out of many shall return,
If we may learn from this day's evidence to trust
Divine prophecy, which shall surely be fulfilled
To the last jot. Therefore those hopes are vain with which
Xerxes now leaves behind the choicest of his men.
Where the Asopus spreads his precious streams to enrich
The dry Boeotian plain, they wait; and there wait too
Ruin and untold pain, which they must yet endure –
The just reward of pride and godless insolence.
Marching through Hellas, without scruple they destroyed
Statues of gods, burned temples; levelled with the ground
Altars and holy precincts, now one heap of rubble.
Therefore their sacrilege is matched in suffering.
And more will follow; for the well-spring of their pain
Is not yet dry; soon new disaster gushes forth.
On the Plataean plain the Dorian lance shall pour
Blood in unmeasured sacrifice; dead heaped on dead
Shall bear dumb witness to three generations hence
That man is mortal, and must learn to curb his pride.
For pride will blossom; soon its ripening kernel is
Infatuation; and its bitter harvest, tears.

      Behold their folly and its recompense; and bear
Athens and Hellas in remembrance. Let no man,
Scorning the fortune that he has, in greed for more
Pour out his wealth in utter waste. Zeus, throned on high,
Sternly chastises arrogant and boastful men.
As for my son, since Heaven has warned him to be wise,
Instruct him with sound reason, and admonish him
To cease affronting God with proud and rash attempts.

      You, my dear wife, his mother, go into the house,
Fetch seemly clothes, and go to meet him; those he has
Hang round him, tattered shreds of royal finery,
Torn in his anguish – all that grief has left to him.

Speak to him words of kindness; for your voice, I know,
Alone will claim and calm him.

Now I must return
Into the nether darkness. Councillors, farewell;
And let your soul taste each day's pleasure, spite of griefs;
For all abundance holds no profit for the dead.

Exit GHOST OF DARIUS.

CHORUS: What bitterness to hear the countless sufferings
Which now afflict, and still await, the Persian race!

ATOSSA: O hand of God! My heart is sick with many griefs;
Yet none more sharp than this, to hear how wretchedly
My son is clothed, to his dishonour. I will go
And fetch clothes from the palace, and prepare my heart
To meet him, and not fail him in his hour of need.

Exit ATOSSA.

CHORUS: When our good king Darius, aged, all-powerful,
Invincible, ruled like a god over Persia,
Then splendour and wealth adorned our city;
Our armies won for us fame in the world's eyes,
Our laws were a tower to protect and guide the State;
From battle our men returned without loss, unwearied,
Victorious, to their homes.

How many towns he captured, without crossing
The River Halys, or leaving his native soil!
Close to the Strymon's mouth and the Thracian settlements
Numerous island States, and the mainland towns
Ringed with stone, acknowledged him lord;
The cities that proudly gaze over Hellespont,
Remote Propontis, and the Northern Estuary;
The islands fringing the sea-drenched headland
On our westward shore – Samos, garden of olives,
Lesbos and Chios, Paros and Myconos, were his,
Naxos, and Andros lying close to Tenos.

Darius ruled moreover the seaward islands
That lie midway between Europe and Asia: Lemnos,
Icaros, Rhodes, Cnidos, the Cyprian towns
Paphos and Soli; and Salamis, daughter
Of the dreaded name that is cause of all our tears.

In Ionia too those rich and populous Hellene cities
Darius ruled according to his own desire;
And, mingled of every race,
An unwearying force of warriors moved at his word.
Now God has proclaimed his will and reversed our for-
    tune:
War and the sea have shattered and conquered us.

> *Enter* XERXES, *his clothes torn; one or two*
> *soldiers attending.*

XERXES: Weep for the deadly doom that Fate
Has launched against me unforeseen.
How bitter to our race have been
The blows of Heaven's savage hate!
Where may I turn to hide my head?
My trembling limbs have lost their use
At sight of these grave men. O Zeus!
That Death had wrapped me with the dead!

CHORUS: Alas for Persia's honoured name!
Alas for all that noble host,
The flower of manhood, Asia's boast,
By gods condemned to deadly shame!
Our land bewails the men she bore,
Slaughtered for Xerxes, who has fed
Hell's hungry jaws with Persian dead;
Lords of the bow, their country's pride,
They followed the dark road and died;
A thousand thousand are no more.
Alas, alas, our country's lord!
That strength in which we placed our trust,

Broken before the Hellene sword,
Has bowed the knee and bit the dust.

XERXES: Behold me, theme for sorrow,
A loathed and piteous outcast,
Born to destroy my race.

CHORUS: We welcome your returning
With inauspicious music,
With Oriental mourning,
And veiled and tearful face.

XERXES: Sing loud in lamentation
Notes plaintive and discordant;
Fortune and Joy have left me,
And Sorrow takes their place.

CHORUS: In reverence for your anguish
And for our fleet's destruction,
We sing our lamentation
Till heart and voice are sore,
With tears and groans that echo
A mother-country mourning
Her sons who went to war.

XERXES: Ionia despoiled us,
Strong in her metalled warships;
But Ares helped her more
To reap the bloody harvest
Of that ill-fated shore.

CHORUS: Come, ask for the whole story.
Where are the stalwart fighters
Who stood at your right hand?
Susas and Pharandaces,
Agdabatas and Psammis,
Dotames, Susiscanes,
Lords of our own dear land?

XERXES: There by the shore of Salamis
I left them, where they fell
Dead from their ships, and floating,

Crushed on the craggy boulders
    By the soft sea-swell.
CHORUS: Alas! Where is Pharnuchus,
    Seualkes, Ariomardus,
        All princely men and bold?
    Lilaeus, Memphis, Tharybis,
    Hystaechmas, Artembares?
        Why leave one grief untold?
XERXES: Alas! Near hated Athens
        They lifted up their eyes
    And saw her ancient ramparts;
    Each man who saw her trembled,
    And plunged to death despairing,
        And there for ever lies.
CHORUS: And your most trusted servant
    Who numbered all your armies,
    Batanochus'* son, Alpistus,
        Is he among the lost?
    Is there more grief for Persia?
    Parthus and great Oebares –
    You left them there, you left them
        Rock-ravaged and wave-tossed?
XERXES: Cease your tormenting questions;
    You tear my heart with yearning
        For every noble friend.
CHORUS: Still others we would speak of:
    Xanthis, who led the Mardians,
    Diaexis, and Anchares –
        Why does not one attend
    His royal master's chariot?
XERXES: They all were Persia's leaders;
        And all have met their end.
CHORUS: Their cruel, nameless end!
XERXES: Break, heart; flow, tears, for ever.
CHORUS: O stroke of Heaven unlooked-for,

Clear as the cruel anger
    That barbs a Fury's glance!
XERXES: An age will not unfasten
    The chains of this mischance!
CHORUS: We are, in truth, defeated.
XERXES: Who could foretell such anguish?
    The seamen of the Hellenes
        In Persia's evil day
    Brought forth their ships to battle,
        And took our pride away.
XERXES: To lose so great an army!
CHORUS: Dead is the power of Persia.
XERXES: See, here, these rags, the remnants
    Of royal robes I wore;
    This quiver for my arrows —
CHORUS: Is this your kingly treasure
    Saved from so vast a store?
XERXES: All dead are our defenders.
CHORUS: And Athens' men are warlike,
    And fierce the deeds they do.
XERXES: I watched the battle, speechless —
CHORUS: When all our ships were routed?
XERXES: I saw that deadly horror,
    And tore my robe in two.
CHORUS: What can we say for comfort?
XERXES: No word can match my anguish.
CHORUS: Twofold and threefold sorrow —
XERXES: While those we hate rejoice!
CHORUS: Our manly strength is crippled.
XERXES: My chosen guards have vanished —
CHORUS: Drowned in the sea that slew them.
XERXES: Let tears drown every voice!
    Go, go to your homes.
CHORUS: Weeping we go.
XERXES: Cry aloud,

Beat your breast for me.

CHORUS: Sad favour, sad request.

XERXES: Join my mournful hymn.

CHORUS: Otototototoi!
O grievous hand of Fate!
O king, we weep for you.

XERXES: Beat your breast,
Groan aloud for me.

CHORUS: O king, behold my tears.

XERXES: Cry aloud, beat your breast for me.

CHORUS: With good will, my master.

XERXES: Cry aloud and groan.

CHORUS: Otototototoi!
Bruising blows mingle with wails of grief.

XERXES: Come, beat your breast, intone a Mysian dirge.

CHORUS: O pain, O pain!

XERXES: Pluck for my sake the white hair from your beard.

CHORUS: With fingers clenched, and bitter cries,
We pluck the white hair from our beards.

XERXES: Weep and howl.

CHORUS: We weep and howl.

XERXES: Tear your gowns, tear them through.

CHORUS: O pain, O pain!

XERXES: And tear your hair in grief for all our army dead.

CHORUS: With fingers clenched, with bitter cries,
We tear the white hair from our heads.

XERXES: Fill your eyes with tears.

CHORUS: Our eyes are filled with tears.

XERXES: Beat your breast, groan aloud for me.

CHORUS: Alas, alas!

XERXES: Go weeping to your homes.

CHORUS: Alas, alas!

XERXES: Let weeping fill the city.

CHORUS: Alas, alas!

XERXES: Weep as you go, with solemn steps.

CHORUS: Every step remembers
   Persian soil dishonoured.
XERXES: Alas, the men who perished
   In our three-banked galleys!
CHORUS: Come now, our lord and master,
   With tears we will escort you
   Home to your mournful palace.

NOTES

The following Notes explain only a few of the references to characters, places, and events in ancient mythology which occur on almost every page of these plays. The Notes in other volumes in this series may give some further help; but in general the reader must be referred to easily available works such as Robert Graves's *The Greek Myths* or Rose's *Handbook of Greek Mythology*, or any good Classical Dictionary.

*

PROMETHEUS BOUND

P. 20 *Dragging in Prometheus.* There is disagreement as to whether Prometheus was visibly impersonated by an actor, or represented by a dummy figure with a mask-head through which, once it was fixed in position, an invisible actor spoke from behind. Such a device would make it possible for the binding and piercing to be more realistic.

P. 28 *For that I am subjected* ... Notice that Strength and Hephaestus implied that Prometheus was punished for stealing fire from heaven, not for preserving the human race from destruction. Prometheus' words here raise the question: Is he deliberately falsifying the story to his own advantage? This would seem to be Aeschylus' intention. Certainly later in the trilogy the case for Zeus was strongly presented; and Aeschylus has here given Zeus a telling argument: the human race, as everyone knows, is full of faults; blame Prometheus; my intention was to destroy it and create something far superior.

P. 33 *The peoples of Europe mourn.* Part of a line is missing in the MSS at this point; this phrase gives the probable sense.

The warlike princes of Arabia ... *near Mount Caucasus.* I quote from the commentary of Sikes and Willson: 'Aeschylus' geography is so chaotic that we can scarcely be surprised at any misplacement, or condemn any vagary as really beyond his capacity.'

Only once before ... *and groans.* The text of this passage is corrupt. It is possible that these lines are an interpolation. If they are omitted, the last stanza of this ode ('And the wave ... for his pain') would refer not to Atlas but to Prometheus. In that case they should read as follows:

> And the wave of ocean roars in unison,
> The depths ... etc.
> Weep in pity for your pain.

P. 37 *The clear music of wax-bound pipes.* At this point the playing of pan-pipes is heard, perhaps to represent the hum of the gadfly; Io takes it for the playing of Argus the herdsman.

P. 40 *To wander homeless.* The literal meaning of the Greek adjective is 'let loose'; and its special application is to animals dedicated for sacrifice to a god and allowed to roam untethered in pastures attached to the temple. Hence its appropriateness to the 'dedicated' Io.

P. 45 *Adriatic.* Literally, 'to the great Gulf of Rhea'. This, like 'Ionian Sea', was an early name of the Adriatic.
Lusting for an unlawful love. Literally, 'intending to pursue a union which ought not to be pursued'.

P. 46 *Beating against waves* ... The image is that of a swift stream meeting the sea.

P. 48 *Speak humbly, and fear Nemesis.* Literally, 'Wise are those who bow down before Adrasteia.' Adrasteia (the Inescapable) is a less familiar name for Nemesis. 'To bow before Adrasteia' meant seeking to avert, by some gesture of humility, the evil consequences of boastful speech.

P. 51 *Till some god be found* ... This prophecy refers to Chiron the Centaur. When Heracles unintentionally wounded him with a poisoned arrow, the pain was so great that Zeus granted his request to be allowed to end his immortal life and go down to Hades.

THE SUPPLIANTS

P. 55 *The Calf whom Zeus begot* ... For the whole story of Io see the Introduction.

P. 56 *Cheeks the Nile has ripened.* The Danaids, as being Egyptians, are dark-complexioned.

P. 57 *The strong desire of Zeus* ... Literally, 'It is not easy to track out what Zeus strongly desires,' i.e. his purposes are mysterious.
Apian. An old name for Argive. Its origin is obscure.
My Tyrian veil. The Greek word is 'Sidonian'; but 'Tyrian' is more likely to mean something to English ears.

P. 59 *These festal gods.* The gods mentioned as visible on the stage are

Zeus, Apollo, Poseidon, and Hermes, all being gods associated with the great 'games' or athletic-religious festivals.

P. 60 *The Isthmian god.* Poseidon.

P. 61 *An invested envoy.* Literally, 'bearing a sacred wand', i.e. a herald's sign of office.

P. 62 *How can a race like yours be Argive?* The fact that the king asks this, instead of 'How can you be descended from a cow?', is funny to us; it may have been to the Greeks; but there is no evidence that it was found so in this passage.

P. 64 *What girl would buy . . .?* i.e. with her dowry. The meaning is made plain in the next two lines. The union of two branches of a family strengthens the family by joining inheritances; but the position of the wife is weaker when she has not a separate family of her own to support her in any dispute with her husband or his family.

P. 65 *If you respect the suppliant . . . altars of the gods.* This is Tucker's conjectural restoration of a passage where some words are missing.

Liable to guilt herein. I.e. liable to guilt in case they fail to fulfil the obligations laid on them by the suppliants' claims.

You are the State. This is in answer to the king's statement, 'This is not *my* house.'

P. 67 *Like a hull clinched with winches.* In boatbuilding it seems that the planks were sometimes tightened about the frame with ropes, to hold them in position for nailing.

P. 68 *Ornaments.* Votive-tablets.

That word falls . . . The king's distress is the result not of pity for the Danaids but of horror at what such pollution would entail for himself and his people.

P. 69 *Inachus.* The first king of Argos, father of Io.

To show your need . . . I.e. to indicate that you have not abandoned your position as suppliants, but are merely moving to the orchestra for the next Ode.

We obey you. Literally, 'We leave them, instructed by your gesture and words.'

P. 71 *The 'freight of Zeus'.* This may have been a proverbial phrase used of a lucky ship.

P. 72 *To perform an act . . .* The act is of course that of rescuing the Danaids.

P. 74 *Artemis of the arrows.* The death of women in childbirth was said to be caused by the arrows of Artemis.

P. 75 *Gunnel-screens.* 'They were a kind of curtain of skins or hair put round the sides of the deck as a protection both from weather and the enemy.' – Tucker.

P. 78 *My father's watching caught.* Watching is the activity of a hunter. The Greek word for 'catch' can also mean 'destroy'.

P. 83 *Any secret murderous stroke.* In the next play it is Danaus himself who will turn murderer.

Take place of honour in our hearts. Literally, 'we should set gratitude to them in a more honoured position in the stern of our mind.' The stern is the place of control, and therefore of honour, in a ship. This metaphor, easy to a Greek, is almost impossible to translate.

P. 84 *When Aphrodite finds ...* The line is very corrupt. This is Tucker's conjecture – not more nor less convincing than several others.

SEVEN AGAINST THEBES

P. 88 *Sons of Cadmus.* Cadmus was the legendary founder of Thebes, and his city was first called Cadmea. In the fifth century the Cadmea was the acropolis of Thebes, and was taken to have been the original walled city. Throughout this play Aeschylus avoids the name Thebes, which was in bad odour with the Athenians; for at the Battle of Plataea in 479 B.C., twelve years before the production of this play, a Theban force fought on the side of the Persian invaders. Aeschylus in using the name Cadmea not only helps to establish the period of his play, but avoids a name offensive to his audience. The name *Seven Against Thebes* was probably not the name under which the play first appeared, but it is used by Aristophanes some sixty years later.

P. 89 *Our prophet.* Almost certainly Aeschylus here means Teiresias, whose life, according to the legends, seems to have lasted over some seven generations.

P. 90 *O Curse of Oedipus ...* Literally, 'O Curse and powerful Erinys of my father.' The word Erinys (plural Erinyes) is used frequently in this play. An Erinys was conceived as a supernatural being connected with the idea of retribution, a 'spirit of revenge or vindictiveness' inherent not in humans but in the moral order. 'The Erinyes' are represented (notably in the *Oresteia*) as hideous and loathsome females, black-robed and winged, who pursue and torment those guilty of certain special crimes such as matricide. Thus if a father curses his sons, as Oedipus did, the Erinyes are the natural agents to ensure the operation of the curse. The Erinys of an individual (which is the sense chiefly used in this play) is less clearly conceived as the 'evil genius' or fiend which on behalf of a wronged person pursues those guilty of the wrong.

Exit Eteocles. There are indications in the text that at this point the scene changes from the Agora or meeting-place to the Acropolis, and at Eteocles' next exit (p. 97) back to the Agora. In an English production, however, all the essential features can well be represented in one scene.

P. 93 *Queen Athene*. The Greek has here not 'Athene' but 'Onca'. This was the name of a goddess, originally Phoenician, who at Thebes was identified with Athene, and had a temple outside the city near one of the gates (see p. 102).

P. 94 *The stone of death*. This refers to the system of voting for condemnation or acquittal by dropping a black or a white stone into an urn. In the following sentence there is a play on the two kinds of 'stone' which cause death.

The shriek of the axles . . . that curb them. In this passage the things described are the wheels and the harness of a chariot, and the sounds they make as they pass; the images used to describe them are musical pipes (the same word, *syrinx*, is used for a pipe and for the cylindrical hole in the nave of a wheel) and the steering-gear of a ship, whose terms are applied to the bridle and bit of a horse. In English the whole effect is impossibly complex; but to a Greek all these were things of daily familiarity, and a 'rudder for horses' was as immediately vivid as a 'bridle for ships'. The translation gives the meaning in a comprehensible form, but can hardly attempt to do more than hint at the interweaving of imagery.

Pray that our walls hold firm. Here the nautical metaphor is used again. The word for 'to hold firm' means 'to be watertight', and the word for a spear also means a keel; so the image is that of one ship ramming another.

P. 96 *You speak such words*. 'If their city's captured' is an indiscreet mention of disaster which in itself makes disaster more likely, and is an affront to the gods whose help is sought.

P. 99 *He runs as fast* ... Literally, 'urging with haste the conveying axles of his feet'. Whether to Greek ears such a characteristic phrase sounded serious, excited, poetical, or faintly humorous, it is probably impossible to say.

The prophet, son of Oecles. Not, of course, Teiresias, but Amphiaraus (see p. 105).

P. 100 *Chariot-horse.* The comparison is with a chariot-race, not a battle. In the next line but one the 'barrier' is the pole behind which the horses waited, and whose removal was the start of the race.

The Sown Men. When Cadmus first came to the site of Thebes, he killed a dragon which guarded the place. At the command of Athene he sowed its teeth in the ground, and from them armed men sprang up, and fought each other. The survivors helped Cadmus to found his city, and were ancestors of the Theban aristocracy.

Capaneus. The name suggests the word *kapnos*, 'smoke' – a common image for ineffectual words. This meaning also hints at his end: during the assault he was struck by lightning.

P. 101 *By the grace of Artemis.* Why Artemis is specially named is not clear. The Electran Gate may have been sacred to her, or Polyphontes may have been her priest.

P. 102 *Athena Onca.* See note on page 93.

P. 103 *Almost flame.* Literally, 'brother of fire'. The *locus classicus* for this close interest in engraved or inlaid metal-work is of course the Shield of Achilles, in the 18th book of the Iliad.

The boast is Panic Rout. 'Rout' seems here to be personified. The meaning is that Hippomedon's vivid boasting has almost made rout a reality.

P. 104 *Not maidenish like his name.* An allusion to the name Partheno-paeus. *Parthenos* means 'maiden'. He was the son of the maiden Atalanta.

Hammered outside in. The figure of the Sphinx is embossed; the Greek word means 'hammered out' from the inside of the shield. Now in the fighting the process is to be reversed, and the spears of the Cadmeans will 'hammer in' the protruding metal.

P. 105 *That ominous name.* Literally, 'twice dwelling on the name in its ending.' *Poly-neices* means *Much-strife.*

P. 108 *Bring my greaves.* As Tucker points out in his edition, the Homeric warrior always put on his greaves first, since the body-armour hindered stooping. Thus it is clear that while the six champions were on stage fully armed, Eteocles was unarmed. This is important as showing that Eteocles' decision to fight against his brother comes as a surprise to the Messenger; while the Chorus, even if they remember his undertaking to be one of the seven, would assume that he had changed his mind. *Phoebus' hate.* See the fourth stanza of the next choral ode, page 110.

P. 109 *Even unvaliant victory* ... A tightly packed line; expanded, it means: 'The mere fact of victory, even the victory of a coward, shows the approval of the gods; how much more will your victory be approved by them, when your refusal to fight Polyneices is due not to cowardice but to piety.'

P. 112 *Commander of Seven.* Apollo had various associations with the number seven. Tucker suggests that 'Commander of Seven' may have been a rank in the Athenian fleet, and that the nautical metaphor is thus continued.

P. 113 *True to their name.* 'True to name' refers to Eteocles, whose name means 'true glory', as well as to Polyneices, whose name is here inflected as a plural adjective, 'full of enmity'. To render the distinction in English becomes too cumbersome.

P. 114 *That sacred ship.* In thinking of the ship in which souls are conveyed over the River of Death, the Chorus contrast it with the 'sacred ship' which every year sailed from Athens to Delos on a mission of thanksgiving to Apollo for the victory of Theseus over the Minotaur. The name Delos means 'clearly seen'; the island was sacred to Apollo, and only the ritually pure were allowed to land there.

Antigone and Ismene. These twelve lines introducing the sisters are spurious (see Introduction, p. 16). The antiphonal mourning song assigned to them, pages 117–18, may well have been written for sections of the Chorus. The whole ending of the play, from the entry of the Herald, is also spurious.

Who bind their gowns ... Probably this simply indicates women of wealth or social position.

P. 115 *Their arbiter.* i.e. steel – according to the curse.

THE PERSIANS

P. 125 *Whose race was sown in gold*. This refers to the tradition that Xerxes was descended from Perseus, and that the Persian race was named from him. Perseus was the son of Zeus, who descended upon his mother Danae in a shower of gold.

P. 126 *On hempen cords*. I.e. on the bridge of boats which were lashed together with ropes.

P. 131 *Ajax' island home*. I.e. Salamis.
The Isle of Doves. The identity of this island is disputed.

P. 135 *This depth of horror ... mingle with the first*. These lines are very likely spurious. It is obvious that in later productions of this play there would be constant temptation to alter the narrative in order to interest particular audiences. The genuineness of the Messenger's next speech is also suspect.

P. 137 *The streets of Susa*. The Greek has, 'The city of Susa and of Acbatana.'

P. 138 *The Cychrean shore*. i.e. the shore of Greece.

P. 140 *Dearly we loved Darius*. In this invocation Darius is several times called by a variant of his name, Darian.

P. 141 *Our Sultan*. The word used is *Balen*, a Phrygian word for a king.
O King whose loss is mourned ... After this line several lines are hopelessly corrupt.

P. 149 *Batanochus*. This name should be accented on the third syllable.